BELLE
CURVE

CHAUNCEY NELSON

Fulton Books, Inc.
Meadville, PA

Published by Fulton Books 2021

ISBN 978-1-63710-204-6 (paperback)
ISBN 978-1-63710-205-3 (digital)

Printed in the United States of America

Morning Circus

Seven o'clock in the morning was too early to be ducking and dodging people. "Good morning, Mrs. Jackson!" I yelled across the street before stepping into my car. We had a love-hate relationship, mostly hate. My neighbor Mrs. Jackson was a nosy old bag, kept her nose in everyone else's business. I made a conscious effort to be respectful, but this lady constantly did indirect things to aggravate me. I had only been living here for six months. She liked to tell me how much weight I'm gaining or criticize my parenting harshly. This morning, I was not entertaining that shit. Nor would I address her. Mrs. Jackson trotted halfway across the street to exchange insults. There was no time this morning. I hurried my twins along.

"Come on, girls. Mia, pick up your sweater. Stop dragging it all over the dirt and grass!" I yelled. Rushing the girls across the lawn did not deter old lady Jackson from heading over to the car. She had her glasses resting on the edge of her nose with her head tilted downward. Mrs. Jackson may have been an attractive lady fifteen years ago. But, she had a permanent frown that made her look aged and haggard. Mrs. Jackson and my mama went to high school together. It was hard to tell that they were the same age. My mom looked so much younger. When I asked about her, my mom did not say much about her other than she had a jealous streak.

The neighborhood gossip was, several years ago, she caught her husband cheating on her with a young nurse from down the street. The lady went missing, never to be heard from again. Strangely, the husband developed a medical condition where he could not talk any longer. Eventually, he died of unknown causes. Mrs. Jackson has been a bitter old bitch ever since.

Her relatives were from Haiti, so the entire neighborhood thinks she put "roots on her husband and the nurse." That's hilarious to me. That old lady don't know nothing about no damn roots. She is just mean and evil for no good reason. Old women in general are just mean.

Nia hopped up in the car. "Good girl," I said. Nia was such a sweetheart. She was nothing like her sister.

"Mia, fasten your seat belt. Hurry up y'all, we are going to be late," I fussed. I rushed the girls even more. Mia was me as a child. She was my parental challenge. I took one moment to fasten my shoe while giving the girls instructions to check their backpacks for their field-trip forms. As soon as I looked up, Mrs. Jackson, with her surprising athletic ability, sprang to my side of the car. She attempted to open her mouth. I was too quick for her this time. With one foot on the gas pedal, my left arm quickly closed the door in just the enough time. I whipped the car in reverse. "Can't talk now, running late. See you later!" I yelled out of the window. I rolled the window up before she could get a word out. *Bye, Felicia*, I thought as I pressed the pedal down to the floor. It was pretty funny seeing her standing there, looking stupid. I would not be surprised if she went through my trash trying to find something malicious to spread over the neighborhood. All she needed was a lead of something negative, and she would embellish the rest to post on Facebook. Only old people get on Facebook anyway. At least that's what my students say. Mrs. Jackson was just too old to be in drama. The first week that I moved into the neighborhood, she told everyone that I didn't know who my twins' daddy was. Out of respect, I have been trying really hard not to curse her out because she was my mother's age.

Nia sat quietly in her car seat, playing with the string in her little Adidas sneakers. Mia kicked my seat three times. "Li'l girl, stop kicking, my seat," I demanded. I pulled out of the driveway quickly. I wondered how much my daughters picked up on our little feud. They were only six but very perceptive.

We were rockin' to Beyoncé's "Formation." Mia knew every word. She really got involved and started reciting the lyrics "I like my baby hair in afros" as she bobbed her head to the beat. It was too cute watching her sing with attitude poking her li'l lips out. I didn't make it any better. I bated her on, "Sing it, Mia."

Just as I was really gassing her up, the morning fight commenced.

"Momma, tell Mia to give my brush!" Nia yelled. Nia usually defended herself in the fight. Mia usually started the fight!

"Nu-uhn… I didn't take her brush. She telling a story, Mama. It's on the floor, see," Mia said to appease her and me while pointing at the floor in the back seat.

"Stop arguing, you sound like two li'l old women back there."

I pulled up at a red light slightly adjacent to Elite Success Academy, which was a one-hour ride from where we live in Miami Springs, Florida. I reminded myself why I made this long drive daily. I sent my kids to a school in another whole school district. It was a sacrifice sending my girls to an academically accelerated private school on the "other side of town." I loved the quality of resources and teaching although my babies were the minority. I wanted the best for them just as any parent would.

My mama sent me and my brother to the most "hood schools" ever. Of course, there was nothing wrong with being from the hood, but I didn't want my kids having to go through the crazy things that I experienced. The walks through creepy funeral homes or drug-infested corner stores are not appealing as a parent. It's not even safe for kids to walk to school anymore.

My brother, Jerald, and I walked two miles to school during our sixth, seventh, and eighth grade year. It was terrifying. We had to walk past a graveyard that seemed like a mile long. The neighborhood kids had a spooky grave tale for every casket in that graveyard. The property was overgrown with dark tall trees, weeds, and moss everywhere. Some graves were halfway in the ground with the other half sticking out. The unique part of the graveyard was that it had hundreds of empty caskets resting along the fence. They were stacked on top of each other. We thought at any point, a zombie would jump out and attack us or one of us would be stuffed in a casket by a killer. Beyond the graveyard, we had to follow a creepy path along the railroad tracks. It had mounds of rocks piled up like a mountain. Jerald and I had two decisions to make on that path: either (1) we were going to jump on the train and ride it a half mile down the tracks with the other kids or (2) we would be left behind and wait for Hobo Jones to come chase us down the tracks. Both options were frightening. "Jumping the train" was incredibly difficult. Climbing rocks in patent leather shoes was just dumb. Trying to jump on a moving train in patent leather shoes was clear suicide! Lagging behind with Hobo Jones lurking was just as bad. Hobo Jones was known for snatching children and carrying them off in the woods. If he kidnapped us both, who would tell our mom? Jerald would never leave me because he knew my mom would kill him. He thought it was all fun and adventurous. I never understood why we didn't take the bus like normal people. My day started like that for three years.

There was no way in hell I was going to put my daughters through that type of terror. I was happy to drive my babies an hour out of the way for their safety.

I snapped out of memory lane as we pulled into the parking lot. I had to be one of very few African American parents in the entire school.

My assistant principal recommended ESA for my girls, and I was crazy about the idea. Elite Success Academy had the most amazing teachers. Mia's teacher, Ms. Nicholas, was standing there in her long asymmetric skirt and a color-block shirt with patterns of letters and numbers—*so* kindergarten but adorable. Ms. Nicholas was a pretty biracial lady with thick brown shoulder-length hair. She was always so sweet to my girls; I couldn't help but love her. With the biggest smile and open arms, Ms. Nicholas reached for the car doors. "Good morning, Mia and Nia! How are my favorite twins this morning?"

Mia and Nia both rushed to get out of the car without even a hug.

"Ms. Nicholas, Ms. Nicholas. Look at my new shoes," Mia said excitedly.

"I have to find Mrs. Rodriguez and show her my shoes," Nia added while running up the steps.

"Bye, girls. I'm just your mother, no one important!" I yelled with a hint of jealousy.

I could see why the girls liked their teachers so much. Students love teachers who love them!

YEAR ONE

I took great joy in being a teacher. Everything about the occupation said so much. People can never call you dumb because it's a given you went to school and earned a degree.

When I tell people I'm a teacher, I get a lot of respect and even more sympathy. In general conversation, people recognize that teaching is a difficult, thankless job. Most of the time, when I mention that I am a middle school teacher, I get the most empathetic looks ever. They have so many questions. People like to pick my brain on the state of public education, teacher pay, public school vs. private school, etc.

I have been teaching at Pine River Middle School for three years. I have the best principal ever! Not to mention he wasn't bad on the eyes at all.

My first year at Pine River Middle, I was extremely anxious. I was a first-year teacher and had little experience with interviewing and absolutely no experience teaching. I was young, witty, and attractive. I was not experienced like most of the teachers in the field who could speak with knowledge of all acronyms and education buzzwords. I had no idea of an Individual Education Plan (IEP), Professional Development (PD) meeting, teaching standards by strand. I was a complete newbie. On my way to the interview, I prayed that they would see my enthusiasm for teaching rather than my inexperience in the field.

The day of my interview was nerve-racking. I was twenty-five years old and clueless about the politics involved in education. The interview for the teaching position was a group-type interview. I walked into a room filled with at least ninety years of teaching experience combined. There was a huge conference table in the center of the room. To my left was Mr. Lawrence, the principal, two other older women, and a male assistant principal. There was another teacher whom they identified as the department head of social studies.

I was nervous as hell. Mr. Lawrence asked me to have a seat. The only empty seat was the one beside him. He was very kind. I had my little briefcase to make me look professional along with my full-length black suit. The briefcase was empty. The suit was absolutely appropriate for the occasion. It fit like a glove but still exuded professionalism! As I anticipated what types of questions that they would ask me, reality set in. The interview had commenced. The first lady asked me where I attended college and what my major was. As I stumbled through that question that I attended University of South Florida, the other lady added on: how many years did I have with teaching middle school students? I was embarrassed to say that I had never had any experience, so I had to rely solely on my whit.

"Well, I recently graduated from University of South Florida. Although I have never taught middle school, I did intern in a middle school in Miami, where I became familiar with Harry Wong's 'The First Days of School.' I was fortunate enough to develop relationships with students, parents, and staff. During that time, I worked with a targeted group for the year. That particular group of students went from being level 1 readers to level 2 readers within the year. They all grew a level!" Mr. Lawrence stepped in almost to shut the ladies down from asking any additional questions. "Ms. Belle, or is it *Mrs.?*"

I quickly answered, *"Ms.,* not married, sir."

"I'm very impressed with your résumé and even more impressed with how you responded to the question you were just asked." Mr. Lawrence turned to his right and asked, "Mr. Smith, do you have any questions for Ms. Belle?" The assistant principal, who was surprisingly quiet, asked me if I had any experience with dealing with a difficult parent and how I handled that.

I answered the question, "In fact, I did during my internship." After I explained how I resolved the issue and assisted an irate parent, the rest was a breeze. I lacked experience, not common sense.

Mr. Lawrence announced to all, "Well, you are quick on your feet and would bring a fresh perspective to Pine River Middle. So, if you want the job, it's yours!"

I could not believe my ears. I went into the interview thinking it would just be practice for the next interview. I was in shock. "You are offering me the job?" I asked, surprised.

Mr. Lawrence, again with patience, stated, "Yes, we are offering you this position. However, this position is a social studies / civics position."

I could not contain my excitement; as Mr. Lawrence reached over to shake my hand, I jumped up and hugged him like a little kid. Everyone in the room did not know whether to erupt into laughter at my lack of interview etiquette or be suspicious that we appeared to have chemistry. Mr. Lawrence did not mind at all! I thanked him continuously. I also had enough skills to thank the rest of the panel for offering me the job, although I know I only had one real fan in that room, maybe two. The assistant principal was intrigued. I saw him looking, but of course, he was not the alpha male; Mr. Lawrence was. I was so excited about the opportunity.

Mr. Lawrence walked me out of the conference room and gave me a brief tour of the school. It seemed more the size of a high school than a middle school. The school had two floors. He explained that my classroom would be on the second floor. I would be the newest teacher on the team. As he walked me upstairs, I saw a few older teachers. I felt intimidated because they had so much to bring to the table.

School had not started yet, and he wanted me to get to know the staff.

"Mrs. Stanford, this our new civics teacher, Ms. Belle. It would be nice if you could take her under your wing and show her around," he asked. The lady was in her midforties and seemed pretty friendly. She was very direct with the do's and don'ts.

School started at eight fifteen; I had to be in place by eight o'clock. My morning station was at the bus loop.

The dress code was always professional, and parking was in front of the main office. Mrs. Stanford looked me directly in my face.

"Off the record, mind your own business, don't tell people your business, and you are always on the clock as a teacher," she warned.

Mrs. Stanford had been teaching for twenty years. She had seen basically everything. I trusted her when she told me to keep my business to myself.

I found my way back down to Mr. Lawrence's office.

"Mr. Lawrence, I wanted to thank you again for the opportunity. See you 8 a.m. sharp," I said.

From that day on, Mr. Lawrence, Keith as I called him, was my new mentor. He believed in me and my ability to be an effective teacher. I was on an unspeakable high, a celebration. I had dreamed of going to the teacher's supply store and getting every colorful map of the United States and a huge red apple that was actually a pencil sharpener.

Once I got into the parking lot, I called my mama to let her know I got the job. I had been working for the Department of Children and Families, and it was rough. It was refreshing to feed young minds instead of snatching kids out of abusive homes. My mom always thought someone was going to try to kill me. She was right! I had been shot while trying to remove a four-month-old baby from her parents. The baby had a broken femur. I was obligated to take the baby and only had so many hours to do it. The police escort had taken entirely too long. So, I had to remove the child from the home without help. The mother cried but eventually gave me the baby. The dad was the damn lunatic. He watched me put the baby in the car seat then fired two shots at me from the front porch. Thank God he missed. I drove off with the door open on my side. The dad was arrested later. It actually made the news.

My mom would be relieved to know that I was officially a teacher, the molder of young minds.

Mama's phone rang three times before she picked up. "Hey, C, how are you and the girls doing?" she asked. She went on to talk about how my dad was developing early on-set dementia. Apparently, he was seeing children playing in his bed and refused to sleep in it.

I let her continue. It was stressful for her taking care of him. Once she paused, I interjected.

"Guess what, Ma, I got a teaching job. I'm a social studies teacher!" I screamed over the phone.

Mama took a few minutes to process the information.

"Girl, what you say? My baby is a teacher? I'm calling Margret, Rose, Caroline, everybody and tell them my daughter is a brilliant teacher," she bragged.

She was just as pleased with the news as I was. Then she reminded me that working was stressful anyway. The news lasted every bit of five minutes before she ended the call.

"Girl, your daddy trying to take a shower with his damn clothes on again. I'll call you back." She hung up immediately. My dad had an advanced case of dementia coupled with Parkinson's disease. He was not well enough to be left alone for long periods of time. My mom was the sole caretaker. It was exceptionally tough on her.

THREE IS A CROWD

The day was still young, and I wanted to share the news with my boyfriend bestie. So I called Promise to give him the good news. Promise usually picked up on the first or second ring. He didn't answer. I texted him, hoping he would be as excited as I was. He still did not respond. Fuck it. His house was only fifteen minutes away from the school. I went home and took off my suit and got into the shower. Bath and Body Works was my favorite feminine product. Moving briskly, I put on a loosely flowing orange sundress with nothing underneath ("A Florida Special") and put on Promise's favorite perfume, Angel. I almost walked out of the house without shaving, the fuck. I reversed my steps and ran into the bathroom. I could never be that excited that I forget about proper hygiene. I went to the bathtub and raised my dress. For the most part, only low maintenance was needed. I took the razor and went to work, careful not to cut my most tender parts. I had to be squeaky-clean upstairs and downstairs. This was supposed to be a quick in and out.

Finally, I jumped in my car and called his ass once more to let him know I was on the way. He still did not answer. I was a few blocks from his house and had a dreadful feeling in the pit of my damn stomach. It was an old, familiar feeling that something wasn't right. Against my better judgment, I had to be a detective and figure out why the fuck he wasn't answering me. As I reached his street, that gut feeling increased. I saw his black BMW in his driveway. Clearly he was home. I saw an unfamiliar gray Honda Civic in front of his yard but closer to his neighbor's yard. It was like he told that person not to park directly in front of his house. I knew something was wrong for sure then. But, I'll be a fat monkey's ass cheek before I just drive off and let Promise get away with this. This is so typical of his behavior. Punk-ass bitch!

I played the same game; I parked my red Audi down the street so he could not look through the keyhole and see my shit. As I walked up the sidewalk to his house, I contemplated what I was going to say or do to his treacherous ass.

I finally reached the door. Using my index finger, I covered the peephole so he wouldn't know who to expect. I knocked firmly to make sure I had his attention. No one answered or opened the door. I knocked two more times. Still no one came to the door. Taking a chance, I turned the door handle to see if it was locked. And it was! Dammit. I still wasn't done. I walked around the side of his house where he has a laundry room that's attached to the house. It's always open for his boys to come in and out. Just as I thought, he was stupid enough to leave it open. I had to mentally prepare for what I might see. Whatever I had to face, I was gonna see it through. I walked in the crowed laundry room; clothes were all over the floor, but there was a clear-enough path which led to the door in the kitchen. It was dark in the hall. I headed toward the living room first. It was quiet. There was nothing but the television, empty sofa with throw pillows, and mail lying on the coffee table, empty. I had to gather myself for the next venture, his bedroom. Men are so fucking stupid and predictable. Why couldn't he just answer his phone, and we wouldn't be here. His room door was closed. Fuck! I opened the door. There he was, lying in his king-size bed, asleep. Next to him was a brown-skinned female sleeping next to him. I could not see her face because her brown hair was tossed over her face. It was clear his ass was a real cheater! I had a gun in my purse—yep, my damn 9 mm. It was the same gun my dad purchased for me when I went off to college. I had to quickly deliberate if I was going to commit murder and spend the rest of my life in prison. My babies were only three at the time. I could lose everything! I walked slowly out of the bedroom quiet as a mouse. It felt like my heart was torn out of my chest and left on the door handle. I maintained my decorum. I had to pep-talk myself all the way to the kitchen. I felt I was too pretty to take that shit. I had so many fucking options. I'm pretty, smart, and fine as fuck. This nigga must be crazy. How could Promise treat me this way?

I searched the kitchen for a saucepan and sugar. Why waste good grits when simple sugar does a better job? I had to be extra quiet. It took five minutes for the sugar and water to boil to syrup. Hot grits burn, but hot syrup will fry the shit out of you. Just as I was taking the syrup off the stove, I heard his room door open. It was his muthafuckin' ass getting up to go to the restroom. He was still a little hazy from midafternoon sex and sleep. He must have thought that he was dreaming; he called out, "Celeste, is that you? Celeste, what you doing in the kitchen, in my house?"

I didn't say a fucking word. I got that hot-ass pot and threw that shit at him, aiming for the face. He was tall, which made me miss his face. But, I did manage to get the right arm instead. He screamed so loud that he woke his little girlfriend. Promise grabbed his right arm in pain. The girl called his name while I charged him. He screamed to her, "Stay in the room! Don't come in here, this bitch crazy!" Promise tried to grab both of my arms, especially the arm with the hot pot. I wiggled loose and managed to hit his stupid ass upside his head with the saucepan. He then tried to choke me; we were in a full-out fight. I kicked his ass in the balls, which was one advantage of fighting him naked. The bitch came to the door but quickly slammed it shut once she saw we were in hand-to-hand combat. I was angry at her for being there. My anger was more directed at Promise for cheating and thinking he could get away with it. The moment he went down, I could see that he was hurt; the syrup got him. I didn't feel bad for him at all. He couldn't even look me in my damn face. I walked out destroyed. I just thought he would have enough respect for me not to do shit like this. Even if he had to cheat, he could have taken her somewhere else. This was the house where I bring my girls. I picked the worst guy in the world to be the father of my twins. The girls were three at the time. I hated him. I don't even remember walking back to my car. My hair was a mess, and my makeup was smeared everywhere. My dress was all fucked up. Basically we were fighting each other naked 'cause I had nothing on underneath. Stupid bastard! I could not stop crying. I put my purse in the back seat thanking God I did not kill that asshole. I called my mom, and she picked up on the first ring. "Hey, Miss Social Studies Teacher, what you doing?" she asked.

"Ma, I need you to pick the twins up from day care today. I have to get fingerprinted and a background check done," my voice quivered. Both car seats were at the day care. My mom was very perceptive, and she knew her daughter well.

"C, why do you sound like you are crying? And don't tell me no fucking lies either," she insisted.

I couldn't hide it; the hurt was too raw. "Ma, I went to Promise's house to ask him to pick up the girls, and there was a girl over there. We got into a fight."

She took a moment to respond because she absolutely hated Promise and the bitch who raised him. Her disdain for him was fueled by his womanizing ways. According to her, he always did fuck up shit like this. What she didn't know was that I did my dirt too. I was just better at it. So, she felt that he ran all over me.

"Did he put his hands on you? A damn finger? 'Cause I been waiting for his ass to do anything else," she threatened.

The last thing I wanted her to do was tell my brother, Jerald. He was a loose cannon on a day-to-day basis. It wouldn't take much to get him charged! He would go over and end it all; Promise's house would be burned down, and the car would be demolished. I'm not sure what would actually happen to Promise. I knew at some point Promise and I would be on speaking terms again.

I was not going to tell her that he tried to choke me or that I thought about shooting him and his girlfriend. I felt good that I narrowed it down to boiling his ass like eggs. She didn't need to know that either.

I answered her, "No, ma'am." I don't know how the happiest day of my life turned out to be the most disappointing day ever. She ended the call with, "I will go pick up the girls. Just take care of your business and don't take your ass back over there. You gonna have both of us on the six o'clock news."

My face was red from the tears and sniffling. I looked down at my dashboard and saw that I desperately needed gas. Although I was in no mood, I had to stop by the corner store to get some gas. I was riding on empty and did not even know it. I was so upset about Promise's stupid ass. As I sat in my car trying to get myself together, I saw a handsome tall figure walk past my car. Even if he looked like Idris Elba, I was not in the right headspace to talk to anyone. I could not risk anyone seeing me look busted. I pulled the mirror down in the car and straightened my hair. A napkin sat in the seat of my car. So, I used it to wipe my eyes and face. It took about five minutes to pull it together. As I stepped out of the car, I heard a man's voice say, "My, I love a bow-legged woman."

Under normal circumstances, I would have played into that compliment. I was just not feeling that shit.

I stood there with the gas pump in my hands for another five minutes replaying throwing hot sugar on Promise. It scorched the shit out of his arm; he deserved it! I got a little satisfaction out of that.

I felt hurt and vulnerable. A gentleman, the same one who passed by my car, came up to me with a tissue. The look on my face must have said it all. He handed it to me with advice. "Any man stupid enough to make a woman like you cry is a damn fool," he said.

It caught me off guard. In my head, I could not erase the image of Promise in bed with another woman.

This guy was well-groomed down to the shoes. He had a goatee that complimented that caramel-chocolate skin. His eyes were the real showstopper. They were a dark hazel with a hint of topaz in the center. Lord Jesus, he was handsome. A dark brother with that kind of eyes was dangerous. The tape-up around his hairline beard was immaculate. He was a little on the larger side. I like a little something extra to hold me tight. His suit was tailored and well fitted and complimentary to his masculine frame. His cologne was heavenly. I studied him for a few more minutes before I responded with, "That's very presumptuous of you to assume that I'm upset over a man?"

He quickly came back with, "Let me take you to dinner so we can talk about it, or not."

On a good day, I may have entertained him, but not today. Clearly, I wasn't in a social mood.

"I'm not up for meeting, dating, dinner, or anything else at this time, but thanks," I responded.

I thought to myself, this was all too confusing. Promise had me all fucked up.

"Maybe another time then. See you later, beautiful. And oh, you should think higher of yourself than to pass up an opportunity like me," he said with a smile.

Six Foot Two walked back toward his car. He returned to his midnight-black Jaguar and began to pump gas. It took me a minute to reflect on what he said. *What harm would it do to give a handsome brother a chance?* I asked myself. So, with that, I walked over to his car.

"What's your name, Mr. Opportunity?" I said in good humor.

"Kade is the name, and I'm glad that you thought about your future before I drove out of your life," he stated overconfidently.

"Well, Kade, give me a call sometime tomorrow," I responded. Kade was a sexy-ass name, damn! One good thing came out of this fucked-up day.

LASTING IMPRESSIONS

Teaching three years made me somewhere between a novice and an expert. Any educator knows that first year of teaching is a survival year. The second year, we pick up a few tricks to learn policy and procedure. Year 3, we get to really embrace the content.

I changed my suit three times. Looking nice for work was never ever an option. Eighth-grade students can be quite blunt if you're caught off guard. They were brutally honest. They let you know when they hate your shoes, if your hair is out of place, or if your clothes are outdated. I had settled on the bright-yellow sheath dress with cap sleeves. It was fitting and professional. Just as I was complimenting myself in the mirror, I caught a glimpse of the news.

"Nia, get the remote and turn my TV up, please," I asked.

"Breaking news, seventeen-year-old shot and killed by the police who stated he brandished a gun. The police claimed self-defense. However, no weapon was found at the scene."

I was so upset. It's a new lynching. All a white cop has to say is "Stop resisting, he's got a gun." Oh, and one of my favorites is when they say, "I saw a suspicious black man... I feel threatened." I could honestly say that I was angry. It's hard to teach eighth-grade students without bias when the topic "the state of Black America" is jacked up beyond recognition. Police brutality was at an all-time high, and it wasn't being addressed. As a black teacher, I was responsible for social studies lessons through real-life experience.

I needed a minute to just relax. After letting my mind focus back to work, my entire mood changed. I had to switch up my lesson plan. I was going to teach a basic lesson on the three branches of government when black and brown boys were dying at the hands of the police at an alarming rate. *If I don't, who will?* I thought. Too many things were going on in the news with young black men being killed by police, neighbors, white men in general. It's like "open season" on killing young black men for no reason at all. I felt like we have been transported back into the 1950s all over again but in living color. Young men can't even wear a hooded sweatshirt without arousing suspicion. How do I prepare a lesson about *unequal justice and proud white privilege without sounding one-sided?* I could not get my mind together after seeing a child murdered for the third time this week.

I walked to the driveway to enter my car. I saw Mrs. Jackson staring in my direction. She did not come over this time. Thank God! I got into the driver's side and then pushed the start button. To my surprise, the car did not start. I tried a second time and still no power. This was the wrong morning for this. It was convenient that Kade stayed the night with me. Who could have imagined that sad afternoon at the gas station would lead to a three-year relationship. Kade understood me in a way that no other man did. I loved that about him. He was a handsome young black attorney. There was not an arrogant bone in his body.

He was caught up in the breakfast routine taking the dishes off the table and cleaning up breakfast plates.

"Damn, babe, you look good in that yellow. I might have to make you late for work," he said.

I quickly responded, "Boy, not today, stop playing!"

"Baby, my car won't start and I have to get the girls to school then get to work," I explained. Kade threw on a polo shirt and went to get his shoes. He was such a sweet man. Kade cooked like a chef, worked hard, and helped me pay bills. He spoiled me and my girls rotten. This man was close to perfect. We almost had it all. The sex was good. But, it was missing something. That was a problem.

While Kade got the girls in the car, I locked up the house. I had one hour to change my lesson. Ninety-six percent of my students were African American. They did not know any of their own history: Emmit Till, Alabama bombings with the four little girls, Little Rock Nine.

Kade started the engine. I jumped in the car and went right in on the conversation about the seventeen-year-old who was shot. We talked about how this was becoming the new norm.

"Mama, why did the police shoot that little boy?" Mia asked.

"The police said the little boy was a threat and felt his life was threatened," I responded.

"The police was scared of a little boy. Did he die, Mama?" she inquired.

"Yes, baby, he did," I said sadly.

Kade stopped the car in the drop-off circle.

"Be good today, pudding face," Kade said to Mia. Then he gave Nia a fist bump and said, "Baby girl, go show the world your brilliance."

The girls loved Kade, and Kade loved them. He never tried to overstep his role as a father figure. He had always been there for us. We were already late. So, I made sure the girls had their book bags and lunches.

"Mia and Nia, I love you guys. Have a great day at school," I said. Normally, I need a little trick daddy to get my mornings started, but it was a somber morning. Kade was more of a neo-soul-type dude anyway. So, Jill Scott it was!

On the way to school, I had to think quickly what I needed to present my lesson on the new black history. It was a relief that our school started an hour later than the twins' school. It gave me time to get to work and set up.

Kade pulled into the parking lot just as Mr. Lawrence was getting out of his Tahoe truck. Kade is such a gentleman; he got out of the car, opened the door for me, and helped me out. He kissed my forehead and handed me a fifty-dollar bill.

"Have a good day, babe, order you some Door Dash since you don't have your car. I have to get to work," he said. He looked over and saw Keith. He gave the street nod for *hello*. Keith lifted his briefcase out of his truck, gave Kade a look of competition. He did nod back.

Kade drove off. I was close to the steps; Keith came up behind me and greeted me with pettiness.

"So that's your li'l boyfriend or whatever," he asked cynically. Of course, I was not going to respond or bring any attention to myself as I entered the building. I continued to the elevator.

Next door to me was an exceptional teacher and friend, Mrs. Nikki Price. We went to college together. Actually, Nikki, Coia, and I went to USF. There wasn't a history fact that she did not know. It was amazing how a student could yell out a year, and she could quote the president at the time, state of America, and the financial state of the country without hesitation. Nikki was an English / language arts teacher. Our classrooms shared an adjoined closet. It was huge and sometimes very creepy. I walked through the closet and knocked on the door. Nikki was just a great teacher, but a really good friend. She was a nice-looking brown-skinned lady who dressed the part of a teacher every day. She was a member of a distinct sorority because she had pearls and décor sprinkled over her classroom. It promoted a "college-going" culture. It was a great conversation starter as well. It was more her thing than mine.

I remember we almost fell out when she pledged her sorority. Our friendship survived it, but it took work. She wanted me to pledge with her, but I refused. I didn't have the mindset to be hazed or used. I just could not do it. On top of that, the girls were so snobbish and unfriendly. I attended a few of their study halls and stopped. That's when Nikki and I started butting heads.

I knocked softly on her door. I knew she was there. When she opened the door, I was surprised to hear Jay-Z playing in the background. She had a smile on her face as if she had been enjoying her music.

"What's up, Nik? I wanted to get your opinion about something academically related," I said. She went over to her desk and turned her music down while asking me to have a seat. Nikki was in her early thirties, a poise-sophisticated lady who had a deadly shoe game.

"Hey, how are the girls? Tell them Auntie has a present for them. But, anyway, what is it you wanted to ask?" she inquired.

I had to organize my thoughts because so much was swirling around in my brain. "Well, with the police shootings on our black men and children, I felt or feel we as teachers need to address this issue," I expressed. Remarkably, Nikki jumped up supercharged. It surprised the hell out of me. Usually she's more subdued.

"It's a damn shame what's happening to our young men. I'm so sick of this bullshit! Of course I will help," she interjected with excitement. "That's my type of shit. They can learn about this other nonessential garbage another day. What's up? These lawless cowards hiding behind badges make my entire ass hurt!"

Nikki looked at me. "Don't look crazy, I know y'all think I'm the boujee one of the bunch, but I'm socially conscious," she responded.

We both laughed out loud, really loud. I asked her how she felt about combining classes for the next couple of days and coteaching a lesson on civil rights with a reading and writing component so that it covered both of our standards. Nikki was definitely interested in the chance to coteach on such an important topic. Black America was in a perilous state. And, we made an awesome team. She had been in Pine River longer that I had. Nikki told me about the job opening and encouraged me to apply. So, I did.

She prepared a PowerPoint while I created higher-order questions to divide up to each of the groups. Each of the groups had to discuss their questions with their group members. Then they would have to share out with the class. The group who support their position with the most evidence was chosen for the next-level debate. It was a success. The students loved it! It was a change of pace from the ordinary ELA and social studies. Boring old lessons where the students recite the preamble had no appeal or real impact. The kids were completely engaged in discussion. Some were literally arguing their point while Mrs. Price and I facilitated.

The principal even gave us a surprise walk-through while we were in midlesson with reviewing Tamir Rice's unjustified shooting. Accountable talk echoed all throughout the classroom. Mr. Lawrence was so impressed.

School ended at three fifteen. We had a faculty meeting that started promptly after school in the auditorium. Teachers usually gathered in the entrance of the hall before actually getting seated for the meeting. I went inside and sat in the front row not really knowing what to expect. This meeting was called at the last minute.

The atmosphere of a faculty meeting was unique. Faculty meetings were often a gathering for the leaders to discuss what "teachers aren't doing right." On some occasions, we were celebrated. Many times it's information that can be summarized in an email. However, they were mandatory according to our teaching contracts.

Mr. Lawrence started the meeting with housecleaning details as he calls it. We were reminded to have updated lesson plans. That was crazy for me because lesson plans are the cornerstone for teaching. But, I guess it had to be said. He then moved on to making sure to monitor students closely during bathroom breaks because some students are partaking in inappropriate behaviors. As teachers gasped at hot topics Mr. Lawrence discussed, it was clear that many teachers were guilty. He then shifted gears to celebrations. As Mr. Lawrence introduced the first teacher, I looked around the room waiting for her to emerge.

"This teacher is fairly new to us this year. I had the opportunity and pleasure of seeing her and her counterpart coteach the most fascinating lesson on civics and justice," he said with excitement.

He then said, "Mrs. Price, please come up." I clapped for her so loudly that I almost missed my own name. "And Ms. Belle."

We both went up to the front to receive a small plaque that said, "Outstanding work."

Mrs. Price and I high-fived each other and smiled at a job well done. Mr. Lawrence added, "I love to see when teachers take the time to plan and make learning fun for our students. It is our purpose!"

We went back to our separate seats. On the way back to the front row, I could feel eyes glued on me, but not in the good way. I heard a couple of older ladies saying something slick as I passed by. "She not doin' nothing special in her classroom that we not already doin', child boo!" She is basic; I don't see the big deal.

I was still too new to address it, but rest assured, I filed a mental note: "We would meet again."

I left the meeting feeling like an excellent teacher. Teachers don't need a whole lot; we already sacrifice with awful salaries we make. But, knowing that we are appreciated and valued for what we do is EVERYTHING!

ANTICIPATION

Still on a high from yesterday's meeting, I was supercharged, thinking in the car I'm attracted to my principal, and I don't know if it's because he had been so kind to me or because, for three years, he has given me every green light possible to explore. There were other nice-looking teachers that I've seen him flirt with, but I felt we had a different connection. I wanted—I needed—his hands, his tongue, his legs, his everything on me.

That was just a fantasy because tonight it was date night with Kade. He was coming over right after work. I needed to be dressed for the occasion. To resist the temptation, I had to remind myself that Kade was a really good dude. Aside from the fact that he was extremely handsome, he had a great job with the Education Association (union lawyer) as an attorney. It was weird that we both worked for the school system in some form or fashion. The only time a teacher would have to meet with a union lawyer was if they were (1) in big trouble with a legal issue involving a student or (2) fighting for their job against administration. The day I met him, I thought that he was just a brother with a decent job. I had no idea he had a promising career.

I was thankful that my car was drivable today. I dropped my babies off to school and got to work with time to spare.

I had on the most adorable fitting peplum skirt which floated above my knee and right under midthigh. My bowlegs were very defined in this skirt. The puff-sleeve white shirt I wore was appropriate but very telling of my well-formed breasts. Shit, I needed a reduction; they were huge. The perks to all curves were endless and fun! They have gotten me out of many speeding tickets. I think I got a kick out of it. Mr. Lawrence had a look in his face that said so much. His eyes invited me to every one of his sexual fantasies. I was feeling my boss, and it was haunting me.

Mr. Lawrence was five feet, eleven inches of yummy caramel. I wasn't attracted to light-skinned men usually. But, he was certainly the exception. I think he was mixed with Hispanic and Black. It was a lovely mixture. His beard was as smooth and black as the hair on his head. My obsession over this man would not stop.

I had gotten to school a little earlier than usual. As I unloaded my portable cart out of the car, a figure appeared behind me. It was Mr. Smith, the assistant principal; he lifted a heavy cart out of my car so I wouldn't have to bend or struggle in a skirt. *How sweet,* I thought. He opened the door for me to the entrance of the school and rolled my cart in for me.

"Thank you very much, Mr. Smith, chivalry is not dead."

He then commented, "Lord Byron would not agree with you. He thought chivalry died a long time ago."

"Wow, so you know the history?" I asked while impressed by his literary knowledge.

"I do enjoy the subtle and direct melodramatic ways of the 1800s," I added. I thanked him once again then went to check my mailbox. The teacher information room which had the mailboxes and union paperwork displayed was directly across from the main office. I think it was designed that way so that the mean, nosy secretary Mrs. Gladys could spy on who came in and out of that room.

As I walked out, I continued to straighten out the pattern to my peach peplum skirt with the pleated bottom just to make sure I was in order. I instantly looked up and caught the eyes of Mr. Lawrence, the PE coach, two male janitors, and some guy I did not even recognize all admiring the view of my curves. It felt a little weird being watched like that. I ignored it as much as possible and shyly said "Good morning" to each of their gazing faces.

Mr. Lawrence tried to play it off a little by saying, "Good morning, Ms. Belle. You just brightened up the entire building with your peach sunshine." I thanked him with a laugh. In my head, I cheered myself on "Got 'em." I would not make the first move though.

Mr. Lawrence, with all seriousness, asked me to check my email today around lunch. I was curious what it could have been about. I complied and said, "Yes, sir."

The day went by quickly, mostly due to my anticipation of my meeting with Keith. It was ten minutes before the dismissal bell. One of my favorite students asked me, "Ms. Belle, why are you trying to be cute today?" I was slightly embarrassed that she saw me getting dolled up because it wasn't part of the teaching-learning process. But, I had plans. There was no way I would be seen without makeup, matte lipstick, and flawless hair weave. I tried to play it off by sounding hip. I explained, "Destiny, y'all think teachers are supposed to look like old church ladies. Some of us have style. It's nothing wrong with looking cute as long as it's not the only thing you have going for yourself, period!"

She laughed and said, "City girls period with a *t* on the end." We both laughed, and the bell rang. Destiny was one of the smartest eighth-grade students that I have. She was always first to answer questions. Her work was always timely and accurate. I have her tutor other students who struggle with the content. I love her.

It broke my heart when her family had to stay in a hotel a few weeks ago because they lost their home; I made sure she had money in her pocket, and I gave her my personal contact to look for a rental property for a low price. She was so appreciative and has been my li'l school daughter ever since. Every teacher has a schoolkid they claim as their own. Destiny even offered to babysit the twins. I might take her up on that offer.

School ended. I went downstairs to the main office. Mean old Ms. Gladys had left early for a doctor's appointment. I sat in the office and watched the bookkeeper and the PE coaches march out of Mr. Lawrence's office. As I waited, I looked around and saw most of the teachers rush past the office trying to get home. I couldn't blame them. People forget that teachers have kids to pick up from school as well. We don't particularly like to stay after school unless absolutely necessary. I could see outside into the parking lot; it was almost a ghost town. To kill time, I looked down at my phone. I saw that Kade invited me for a movie later tonight. *That was adorable,*

I thought. Finally, Mr. Lawrence emerged from his office looking like a whole snack. He spoke and motioned for me to come into his office.

I got up, gathered my bags and roll cart, and walked into his office.

"Sit down, make yourself comfortable," he said in a professional manner. I straightened out my skirt as I took a seat. He asked how things were going—small talk.

I nervously answered, "Things are good, and I am enjoying the school year so far."

He then asked if there was anything that I needed. The conversation was light, and then he hit me with, "Is there something that I can do to make you more comfortable?"

I took a moment to answer that question carefully. I know what he meant, and the signal was clear. The night janitors were in the hall sawing away at something. The janitors made a lot of noise. Mr. Lawrence asked my permission to close the door. As he attempted to return to his chair behind his desk, he knocked his business cards on the floor. The cards lay dispersed directly in front of me. I volunteered to get them up, but Mr. Lawrence insisted that he get them up. He was extremely close to me.

His five-foot-eleven frame stooped down to pick up the cards. His entire body overshadowed mine. There was very little space between his desk and my chair. His head went low, very close to my thighs. My heart started racing. I am so glad I took a ho-bath in the staff restroom right before I came downstairs. He then got on his knees to get a better angle to gather the cards on the floor. He looked up, straight into my eyes for the okay. Of course I obliged, so I parted my legs slightly to let him inside. Mr. Lawrence took his index and middle finger and slid it gently to the inside of my thighs then between my panties. His touch was so gentle and precise. I slid farther up to the edge of the chair so I could get more of that feeling.

He whispered, "You look like you needed this." He then slid both fingers up and down the tip of my clitoris. I could not scream in desire, so I reached for his chest. It was so firm and hard. He was one fine man with a hell of a touch. I wanted more. I pulled him closer to me so he could match the rhythm of my body. At this point, neither one of us cared about who was in the building. The door was locked.

I grabbed his chin and positioned his head directly up at my face. He didn't have to ask. He wanted a taste. I shook my head yes. He then lifted my legs on both sides of the chair while scooting me back. I was totally exposed with one leg on the left arm and the other leg on the right arm of the chair. Mr. Lawrence then moved my Victoria Pink panties to the side with the same two fingers that used to invigorate me. He bowed his head between both of my thighs. He took both hands and opened me up, sticking his tongue into my middle. I wanted to scream out again even louder, but I grabbed his head instead. His tongue maintained the perfect rhythm for me to climax. I was fucking his tongue, and I loved it. He had a soft, thin tongue like a lizard. He licked the side of my center until he hit the most sensitive part, the top. I felt tingles and icicles taking over my body. He could tell by my leg shaking that he was in the right spot. So he stayed there. He licked and licked until I leaned forward and whispered, "I'm finna cum. Wait, I'm gonna cum." He stopped abruptly. I was confused and trying to catch my breath. I was *so* close to cumming. He took my legs one at a time and placed them back on the floor. He removed his handkerchief from his jacket pocket and wiped his mouth with it. He then wiped his beard before he took the same handkerchief and wiped my thighs thoroughly.

Mr. Lawrence then stood up and said, "I hope you enjoyed that, Ms. Belle, I certainly did. As a matter of fact, when we are alone, please call me Keith. I hope I made you comfortable enough to do that."

I responded with, "Of course, Keith. I enjoyed that very much. I was close to—"

Keith cut me off and said, "I know, but I don't want you to cum yet." He picked up the last business card and sat it back on his desk. Keith returned to his chair and started talking as if nothing had happened.

He then spoke, "I was very impressed by the innovation I saw with your teaching. I think you would be perfect for our after-school program." I was shocked by it all. Cunnilingus and then an after-school job.

I managed to find the words, "That sounds great. Could you tell me more about the opportunity?"

He responded, "I will get you all of the details by the end of the week." I agreed. With a very puzzled look on my face, I collected all my teacher materials and cart. He walked me to the door. As he opened it, he whispered, "Have a great night, Ms. Belle."

I looked up at him and said the only thing I could say at the time, "Yes, sir, I mean Keith."

I left all worked up. Kade needed to be prepared to put some real work in. Fuck a movie! I had to release. Thank God Sequoia was picking up the twins today.

I picked up my phone. I wanted to tell my best friend. But, I did not know how to process what just happened. Before I could call Sequoia, she called me. It was like we both had mental telepathy. The phone rang. "Hey, C, I got the girls. We are on the way to my house," she said.

"Coia, hey, girl. I will be over there later when I leave my meeting. Don't eat anything, I'm picking up two garlic crab trays and wine coolers," I squeezed in.

"Now you are speaking my language. But I did stop to McDonald's to get the girls Happy Meals. Tell Habib to make my garlic crabs extra spicy. Don't forget the sides, shrimp, sausage, eggs, and corn," Coia added. She then hung up the phone.

Sequoia Edwards was not just my best friend but the closest of all my friends. I considered her my sister. We've been friends since middle school. She was there when my babies were born. She knew every secret, every plan, every guy. She could not know about Keith yet. We had a great little school family, and I did not want to fuck that up. Sequoia would have killed me for making such an irresponsible decision. I had been there three years, with an unblemished record. I don't know what finally made me succumb to my desire.

Boo-Boo the Fool

My confidence level was through the roof. Although Keith and I had not had sex, our attraction was undeniable. I tempted him at every opportunity possible. We had to be extra careful not to give ourselves away. He was a private person and I did not need the drama on the job.

It was Friday "play day" for adults. Once a month on a designated pay period, some of the staff would meet out at a local pub for drinks and dancing. I didn't have plans, and I was curious as to where the night would take us. Kade had to work, and the twins were with Promise the weekend. It was a Friday. I did not want to go to any of the raunchy clubs in Miami. I was not up for the type of fun this weekend. Coia agreed to go. That was great news. I would have a partner in crime if shit got uncomfortable. Nikki had an engagement with her husband and could not go. The challenge would be ending the night with Keith without Coia knowing. We drove my car and left her car at school. She was "turnt" and ready to go. It was going to be an interesting night. We were both starving. The golden rule was "Never eat in front of others, especially snooty teachers." They judge you by your weight, how much you eat, what you eat, vegan or keto, even the portion sizes. So, we decided to go get something to eat before going to the pub.

The closest restaurant to the pub was a Jamaican spot. I was ready. We ordered curry chicken, peas, and rice with cabbage. It was delicious. I was *so* hungry. I think I swallowed my chicken whole. Coia had an extra side of jerk chicken with her meal. I could not finish my food. I saved the remainder for the girls. They had advanced taste pallets. We talked and laughed about work. We had been there for about forty minutes.

"Hold on, C, my damn stomach hurts," Coia cried out.

"I told you 'bout that hot-ass jerk chicken. Not smart," I replied back.

"No, I'm serious, you know I had gallbladder surgery. I gotta go to the bathroom immediately," she added. Coia rushed to the bathroom. As she ran to the restroom, I had the chance to text Keith.

C: Are you coming tonight?
K: I certainly hope so.

I put a laughing emoji with a pussycat and a tongue. The next text gave the details of where to meet him after we left the pub. Damn, how am I going to tell Coia? I still wasn't ready for her to know about me and Keith just yet. She would have too many questions that I'm just not ready to answer. I would never hear the end of it.

We got to the pub a little late because Coia couldn't get her damn life together. All the action had kicked off. The building looked run-down on the outside. Yet, the inside was newly renovated. The parking lot was all dirt and grass. We managed to find a spot close to the front. As we entered the bar, the party ambiance pulled us in. The atmosphere was dark, loud, and busy. Some teachers were drinking, playing pool, and dancing on the floor to nineties hits. Others were at tables eating. I perused the room looking for one person. I was just about to find a spot for us to sit when Coia yanked my shoulder hard. "Girl, what the fuck wrong with your crazy ass?" I yelled.

She headed over in the direction of the ladies' restroom. Then Sequoia immediately ran back in my direction. I already knew what was happening.

"Damn, not now, Coia," I said with annoyance.

"I can't help it. The bathroom in here is full, and my stomach won't stop. I gotta go now. I'm just gone shit outside. Won't nobody see me. But, I need you to stand guard," Coia insisted. She and her damn stomach were a disaster. That's why we stop going out as much. Every time she drinks or eats greasy foods, her stomach gets abnormally upset. She had a developing case of explosive diarrhea. How could I leave my best friend in this state of emergency?

It was fairly dark outside. She saw a spot between two large trucks. "Coia, hurry up, what if somebody comes out here?" I commented.

"That's what you here for. Now shut the hell up. I'm in a crisis," she stated.

Coia was trying to balance between two trucks and pull her pants down at the same time. I stood guard as requested. I looked back when I heard something had gone horribly wrong.

"Oh shit, I can't get my pants down," Coia said in distress. I wasn't going back there to help and get shitted on. Hell no, I had places to be tonight. I should have just gotten some KFC and kept riding.

Coia called out, "C, it's coming, I can't hold it no more. I heard a disgusting squirting noise coupled with two loud farts. She shitted all over her jeans and the back of her shoes. It was a runny, diarrhea mess. We had no toilet paper, nothing to clean her up with, just a shitty mess.

"Now what are we supposed to do?" I asked Coia.

The smell was horrid. I was just praying that the crowd stayed inside. We would never be able to live this embarrassment down.

"How the fuck am I supposed to know? I'm covered in shit. Fuck... I need you to go ask the manager if he has a water hose out back," she suggested.

"I can't leave you out here like this half naked," I pleaded.

"Who gon' rape or kidnap a woman covered in human feces? Trust me, I will be right here when you get back," Coia commented.

I ran inside as fast as I could. I unexpectedly ran into Keith at the door. "Everything alright?" he asked.

"Of course, Ms. Edwards just had a little too much to drink. I got it handled," I said in panic. I looked over Keith's shoulder, searching for the manager.

"I can come out and get her to the car for you," he offered kindly.

We were in close quarters. He massaged the side of my breast as I stood beside him. My mind would not let me desire more. I quickly changed the tone of the conversation.

"I wouldn't want her to be embarrassed if her principal saw her like that," I quickly added.

He assured me he would help if I needed it. I wanted to inquire about tonight's plans, but I had to tend to the grown-ass baby outside.

I asked a waitress for a manager. She walked me over to the bar area. I had to be honest with him to get access to the water hose. The manager laughed a little but tried to conceal it.

"I just need to know if we can use the water hose outside, sir," I asked impatiently.

"Of course," he said. He was still tickled. The manager was a chubby white guy with dark hair. He shuffled in the direction of the back of the pub and pointed to a screen door that led outside. The water hose was on the left side of that door. I thanked the manager and went to find Coia. Instead of going back through the pub, I ran the perimeter of the restaurant until I reached the front of the bar, in fuckin' heels. I could have killed her! Coia was still there in between the two trucks with less clothes. She had stripped down to a long shirt and a pink bra.

"Coia, what the fuck?" I asked, confused.

"Look, bitch, you took an entire year in there, and I needed to get out of these shitty clothes. My favorite pants are ruined, *fuck*," she complained.

It would have been funny if I wasn't part of this damn clown show. "Get my clothes. C," Coia requested.

"I wish the fuck I would get them shitty-ass clothes, bitch, never," I said emphatically.

I escorted her crazy ass around the side of the building toward the water hose. She lifted her shirt, and all over her light-brown skin were uneven brown stains sliding down her legs.

"Turn around, I can't get all of it off your leg," I instructed. I did not intend to be looking at her ass and coochie and shit. This bitch needed a bath with soap, bleach, and damn water.

I finally rinsed her bottom half. She was naked from the waist down. I went and got my car and drove around back.

"Hold on, Coia, don't sit on my seat let me get something to sit on," I implored.

"You not right! It was your idea to get damn Jamaican food. Now I'm dying, and you don't want me to sit in your car," Coia whined. She was playing the sympathy card. She sat her bare ass on my seat anyway.

This night was ruined, and I didn't want to prolong it any longer with her stanky ass.

After a long two hours, I drove her back to her car parked at the school. While, I waited for her to get her naked ass in her own vehicle, I texted Keith:

C: Call. DON'T text when you leave the pub.
K: Got it.

PRIVATE PARTY

It was about 9:00 p.m. when I met Keith on the other side of town at a bed-and-breakfast. This was definitely not going to be a breakfast type of deal. I got out of my car first so that I could double-check my clothes and make sure there was no sign of feces on me at all. My mom always taught me to travel with perfume so that I could freshen up at any point. Keith took a little longer to get out of his truck. I wanted to give him space to finish any important calls while I did a makeup check. As his five-foot-eleven frame exited his SUV, I was turned on to another level. He was so fucking smooth, fine for no reason. He removed his jacket and sat it on the headrest of his truck. Keith closed his door. He leaned down as if he had something on his shoe.

I walked over to give him a hug. "Hey, sexy, you made, it," I said excitedly. He was still checking the bottom of his shoe.

"Everything okay?" I asked.

Seemingly frustrated, he said, "I think I stepped in dog shit at the pub when I was getting into my truck. It's fucking up my night."

The first thing I thought was, Coia was between two trucks. They were both dark colored. She shitted beside his truck, and now Keith has it on his shoe. I really hope this is just a coincidence. *This muthafucking night is just a catastrophe*, I thought.

I collected my thoughts and said, "Baby, the last thing that you need to worry about are your shoes. You won't need them."

He smiled, and his mood changed. Keith had the room key, so he headed to the door first. I lagged behind just to see what kind of mess he actually had on his shoe. Yep! It was Coia's shit. He wiped his foot on a mat prior to stepping into the room.

Neither one of us knew how to break the ice. I made it easy for him. As he sat down on the chair close to the bed, I went in front of the mirror adjacent to the chair and bent over so he could get a full view. My bohemian curly hair was clipped in a ponytail on top of my head. I released the hair and let the black curls fall down the middle of my back (twenty-four inches). I was about to give "let your hair down" a whole new meaning. I slowly unbuttoned my sheer blouse and let it drop to the floor. I stood there in my bra and jeans, displaying my round hips and small waist. Admiring my own figure, I removed my bra and threw it in his direction. This revealed my plump peanut-butter-colored breasts with cocoa nipples. I could see in the mirror that he enjoyed the view. Keith leaned back in his chair and got comfortable. He untucked his shirt and loosened his belt, never taking his eyes off me. Still in front of the mirror, I bent all the way over to take off my jeans. I had on black lace cut-out panties with three straps on each hip. Keith took a sip of his Hennessey and Coke, sat it down on the nightstand, and removed his shoes. He approached me from behind. His body towered over mine. He bent me over in front of the mirror and kissed my neck and back. He then began to grind the back of my ass with his pelvis. I felt something stiff and hard behind me. He took two fingers and gently slid them into the side of my panties. Keith worked his way to the center of my clitoris. His fingers slipped up and down my clit as he kissed my ear. I put one knee up on the dresser so that he could travel further in the middle. I began to grind against his fingers to get that stimulating friction. Keith removed his fingers from my panties, turned me around, and folded me up like a pretzel on the dresser. He took both of his large hands and ripped my panties off from the center. Damn, I paid sixteen dollars for these panties, but I guess money well spent. I was completely exposed on the dresser against the mirror. Keith knelt down face-to-face with my shaved vagina. He ran his index finger from my navel back to the tip of my clit. I flinched in pleasure. The external part of my clit as well as the hood began to throb uncontrollably. The clit is the most nerve-rich part of the woman's pussy. It has 8,000 nerve endings. Keith touched every bit of 7,500 of mine. This man must have studied that. "Babe, you feel so good, don't stop," I said as he continued.

Keith went down to kiss my entire middle with his lips. He started at the center and licked his way up using long strokes with his tongue. He sucked my clit slowly and very softly until I grabbed his head. I guided his head to the exact top of my clit. It became a powerhouse of pleasure. He licked and sucked until he achieved the perfect rhythm. My legs were then wrapped around his neck while both of my hands held his head close to my center. I was fucking his tongue. I could feel my hips grinding in a circle to match his rhythm. Ten minutes of this intense feeling, my legs began to shake. I told him, "Keith, I'm about to cum in your mouth, don't stop."

He didn't stop at all. He licked and growled at a low volume. The feeling was more intense; he figured out that circle trick with his tongue was a winner. He circled my clit three or four times in a row when I released so fucking loud. "Keith, babe, I'm *cumming*!" I yelled. I forgot we were in a hotel. I was really noisy.

I had no time to recover from the orgasm. He repositioned me onto the bed. He could not wait. His pants were off. I don't even remember when that happened. I sat on the bed as he faced me standing. I opened my mouth, and he eased his penis in without question. I grabbed both sides of his hips to get a good grip while I swallowed him all the way down to the bottom of his shaft. He grabbed my hair gently and fixed it to the right side of my shoulder so that he could guide me to his pleasure zone. I reached down and ever so gently cupped both of his sex glands in my hand. I let my tongue slide all the way down the shaft and onto his soft glands. He seemed to like that. I gently licked one at a time. I rubbed them softly for stimulation. My tongue reversed direction back up to his penis and completely covered the head. He began to push his rod further inside my mouth. About eight minutes in, he could not take it. Keith was completely hard and turned me over.

"Get on all fours," he said with authority. I obeyed! I scooted to the edge of the bed and bent down on all fours in front of him. He got a great view of this physique and decided to enjoy it for a moment. "Damn, I should take a picture of this ass up in the air like this," he said. Keith took his penis and rubbed it around my flower until he found the precise entrance. He put his dick in the mouth of my flower and eased his way inside. It wasn't big or fat. His dick was on the smaller side, but he knew how to work it. Once inside, he got his grind pattern quickly. He thrust in and out, pausing in between, trying not to cum. He loved being in control. Keith rose up slightly and grabbed the left side of my hair then the right, gathering it in a long ponytail so he could really put some power behind his strokes. "Ooh shit, this pussy is good!" he yelled out. I threw it from the back and round in a circle. He could hardly take it. He repositioned his hands.

He then grabbed both side of my hips. The silhouette of my small waist expanding into my large round hips drove him crazy. I felt him run his arms up and down my frame. Pumped in and out, in and out. He took his dick out and released all over my ass.

Keith went to the bathroom and got a warm washcloth and wiped the cum off my bottom. He then wiped himself down with the same washcloth. I took pleasure in seeing him wipe his mouth and beard. I know all my juices were on his face. We both fell out on the bed. It seemed like we had been intertwined for hours. But, it had only been forty-five minutes.

Keith kissed me as I lay there recovering my strength. That orgasm gave me instant paralysis. He went to shower quickly. By the time I sat up, he was fully dressed.

He had on his clothes, and I was still completely nude. It was obvious that he was about to leave. I stood in front of him almost for approval. He hugged me firmly. My head fell in his chest.

"You are a handful, Ms. Belle," he said. That was plenty without him having to elaborate.

I smiled and said, "I'm guessing that is a compliment."

He bent down and kissed my lips. "Text me and let me know that you made it home," he suggested. He walked out of the door and got into his truck. I was still in the hotel getting my life together. As I got in my car, it occurred to me that I needed to call and make sure Coia was okay. I plugged my phone in the car for a charge and called her.

"Hello," Coia answered.

"I just want to make sure you got your damn life together after the whole bathroom thing," I said.

"Very, funny. You are a damn comedian now. Yes, I'm good. I walked my naked ass right in the house like it was nothing. I took a shower, and I'm good," she said like it was no big deal.

We said our goodbyes, and I continued to head home. I wanted to call Kade just to check in. I would say the wrong thing and tell on myself. I felt slightly guilty for cheating on Kade. But, this was cheating with a purpose. I had the perks of making extra money at work and having great sex. The hotel became our standard meeting place for weeks. We alternated Fridays and Saturdays.

WEEKEND

It was a sunny Miami Saturday, and all I really wanted was to get some rest. Running during the week with the girls and teaching after school became exhausting. I was thankful that Promise was taking the twins for the weekend.

"Mommy, where are my red church shoes?" Mia asked.

"Li'l girl, you don't need church shoes. Just get your rainbow sandals, and please get Hanna. Hurry UP!" I yelled. The last time Mia spent the night with Promise, she forgot her doll, Hanna. She cried for hours until he finally got up at eleven o'clock at night and drove back to my house for that damn doll. The things parents will do for peace of mind or quiet.

"My daddy said he taking us to church with Ms. Angie mama. I need my shoes to match my dress," she begged. I did not want her to start whining. And, it was a reasonable request.

I found her shoes and shoved them in her already-crowded backpack.

This should be interesting, Promise in church. His ass may spontaneously combust. *The devil himself going to church*, I pondered.

Nia was already packed and sitting quietly in front of the TV with her backpack on. She was adorable with her lace socks and favorite book in hand. I just wanted Mia to be calm like her sister.

I looked out of the window, and I could see Mrs. Jackson two houses down speaking with the neighbors. She was probably spreading gossip. Promise pulled up in his pearl-white Escalade thinking he was the absolute shit! Fuck him. I was over that shiny, glittery crap. He did not need to come in my house. Mia was right at the window waiting for her daddy. She jumped down off the sofa, grabbed Nia in one swoop, and hollered as loud as she could.

"Daddy outside! We gotta go, Mommy!"

I walked the girls outside. Promise hopped out of the driver's seat while his Ms. Angie, I guess, sat in the passenger's side eyeing me closely. She studied my face, then she went to my figure. She had a very nasty look on her face. I waved at her, but she didn't wave back. I didn't have ANY interest in Promise beyond coparenting. But, I thought it would be entertaining to give her a show. Instead of saying my goodbyes on the porch, I flaunted my ass to the truck in a halter top and booty shorts.

It was Saturday, and I felt like being a childish baby mama! Ms. Angie wanted a look at the competition, so I gave it to her.

Promise was as ignorant as ever. "Man, watch out. I don't need you to put their seat belts on. I got it. Go enjoy your weekend with Cake, Cabbage, Kade—what's his name," he said sarcastically. He thought that was funny. I didn't! As he picked Nia up to sit her in the truck, I saw the visible burn mark on his arm. I took small pleasure in that.

I didn't say a word. I sauntered back up to my porch. I turned around to make sure that Ms. Angie took it all in. I saw her give him the look of death. Maybe she didn't appreciate the Kade comment. Mrs. Jackson was scrutinizing from across the street. She was really a stalker. She looked at me with repulsion. She rolled her eyes as if she was terribly bothered by my presence. The crazy stalker walked across the street into my yard. There was an Amazon box in her hand.

I don't like this lady. She does not like me! Why does she keep talking to me?

Mrs. Jackson in a raspy voice declared, "The Amazon driver must have gotten our address mixed up. He dropped this on my porch."

She rolled the box on to my hands so fast I almost dropped it. I stooped down quickly with my hands out to catch the box.

"Thanks, but you almost made me drop it," I said frustrated.

She then said, "You should be a lot nicer to your elders, you know that." It took me by surprise. I gave her a sideways glance. She was never nice to me. Why would I ever be respectful to her?

"Maybe I would consider it if you stop spreading gossip and lies about me." I clapped back. She gave me a wicked look. She stood there a second then walked off.

Promise looked at me and thought the entire ordeal was comical. "So this is the new *Love and Hip-Hop in the Ghetto*. You arguing with old bitches now," he said in a hearty laugh.

I politely shot him the middle finger without the girls watching. I wanted his ass gone and Mrs. Jackson, along with his punk ass. They tried to fuck up my Saturday.

That was probably the most excitement I would get that weekend, I thought.

Just as Promise pulled off with the girls, my mom pulled into the driveway. Perfect timing! Those two did not get along. A few years ago when I was in the delivery room with the twins, Promise took hours to get to the hospital while I was in labor. My mom called him while we were on the way. NO answer. She called when we got there and checked in. NO answer. We finally reached Promise's mom and dad. They got out to the hospital immediately. His dad actually wanted to come into the delivery room to take his place. I had my mama and Sequoia; I was good with that. He didn't show up until Mia was about to slide out.

"I just seen your sperm bag drive past me. Was he picking up the girls?" she asked maliciously. I am sure if Mia or Nia had a cheating-ass baby daddy, I would feel the exact same way.

"Mom, I don't like him either, but he's a good dad and the girls love him," I said defensively. We had this entire conversation through the driver's window in the car.

I thought my mama would at least come inside and chat with me. Instead, she said, "I was just passing by and wanted to see my babies. Since they are gone, I'm going to Maxine's house to play Pokeno. You know I can't be gone too long, your daddy may do some ridiculous shit while I'm gone," she complained.

This was a great time for me and Kade to spend some time together. I texted him and told him to pick up something to eat. We could watch Netflix, eat, fuck, and chill—maybe not in that order. He responded that he would be over about seven.

The weekend was never mine. There was a knock at my door. I did a mental head count; this morning alone, I had a total of four visitors. WTF? It was my brother and his entourage. "What is it, Jerald?" I asked.

If my brother came by unannounced, something was up. It would be cool if it were just him. Instead, he brought the entire Miami Dolphins team with him. He would never reveal his true intention for coming over.

"We came over here to make sure my sister was straight! You good, sis? Yes, of course. I know you got something good to eat in the refrigerator," he implied.

"Wash your hands before you go in my refrigerator." They dominated the living room, ate heartily, and talked loudly. Jerald grabbed my remote and turned to ESPN. It was at least thirty minutes that he realized that the girls weren't there. He loved them. And they adored my brother. Kids are drawn to crazy for whatever reason. Jerald was my crazy-ass brother. Everywhere that he went, trouble followed, without fail.

"Sis, I need you to write one of those intelligent emails that can get a muthafucka fired," he explained. We just left the Chinese restaurant over off Twenty-Ninth. So they had a sign outside that said "Lunch Special 6.99, for fried rice, sweet-and-sour chicken, and an eggroll. Okay, so boom! We walked to the counter and ordered. When the shit came back, it was 11.00 per meal instead of the 6.99. I told the Asian lady the price was not calculated right because the sign outside said 6.99. This bitch started arguing with me in English and Chinese. I did hear that crooked-toe muthafucka call me stupid. I kept my cool and went outside to physically get the sign to show them they were wrong. The Asian lady followed me outside. I pointed to the damn sign just in case she did not understand me; "6-9-9," I said, loud as hell. This backward bitch jumped on my mutherfucking back. Out of nowhere, she just jumped on me. I grabbed that same lunch sign and hit her on the top of her head while she was on my back. So I was swinging the sign backward over my head, smacking her with it. I tried to knock her ass out with that shit. The manager had to pull the lady off me. You know I don't fight women, but that bitch deserved a special ass whopping. The manager started yelling for us to leave. They didn't apologize, give us free food, or nothing. People just passed by with their phones recording the whole thing. The moral of the story is, we are hungry and I was attacked. "I need for you to write the news station, Better Business Bureau, and the mayor. They need to know 'bout this bullshit," he declared.

I knew there was a reason he was at my house. The police were probably looking for his crazy ass. But, the Chinese people were dead wrong for that foolishness. My brother and Coia were magnets for this kind of trouble. Unbelievable!

"Jerald, so did they call the police on you?" I asked. I was scared of the answer.

"I can't believe you just asked me that…my own sister. I should be calling the police on them right now. They attacked me!" he yelled.

I was not going to add fuel to the fire today. I needed to calm things down before he returned to the scene of the crime and did something stupid. So, I agreed to write the emails. I wasn't really going to write the mayor though. That was just too much. His friends added to pieces of the story to give me a full picture.

I really thought this would be a low-key kind of day. "Jesus, be a fence." They left three hours and four stories later. Next time, I'm not answering my door.

Kade came over about seven fifteen. He picked up pizza and wine coolers for me. Jerald and his friends wiped me out. There was not a crumb left in the kitchen. Kade got comfortable, and we hung out for the rest of the night.

MY BESTIE

Having a work best friend was fun. But, having my childhood best friend working with me was insanely entertaining. Sequoia "Coia" Edwards was my bestie since middle school days. We grew up together. We used the networking system heavily. During my second year at Pine River, I told her about the opening we had here at the school. I asked Keith to look out for my girl. And, he did just that. She got the job as a reading teacher.

I walked into Ms. Edwards's class. She had three students surrounding her at a "kidney table" shaped like a semicircle in the center of the room. From the door, I could hear one of the girls reading an article slowly, pronouncing each syllable carefully as if she was afraid to say the words incorrectly.

Ms. Edwards attempted to interrupt the little girl, "Lona, didn't I tell you the word is pronounced 'ob-sta-cle'?

"Now, start over from…the fisherman," Coia demanded.

The little girl put her head down in embarrassment. She put her head down as if she was disappointed that she did not perform well for Ms. Edwards.

She continued on a tirade. "Seventh graders should know how to read by now! This stuff is simple," she said.

I walked over to the little girl and put my hand on her shoulder and asked her name. The little girl responded, "Alonna."

"Alonna, you are doing fine, just keep practicing. I'm going to borrow Ms. Edwards for just a few minutes." She shook her head yes, very relieved that I had taken the attention off her struggle to read.

I called Ms. Edwards in the side office that sat in the rear of her classroom. Ms. Edwards walked swiftly to the back office in both frustration and anticipation. Before I could get started, Coia started up once more on her soapbox.

"These damn children making my head hurt! We read this shit three times already, three times. I ain't getting a dime in recognition money messing around with they li'l simple asses," she complained.

I interrupted, "Coia, you are so mean. You couldn't teach my kids or we'd be fighting in the hallways." We both laughed it off, and things got awkwardly silent. "Your damn kids better know how to fuckin' read, that's all I gotta say," she added.

A serious look came over my face, and Coia sensed that something disturbing was going on with me. "Celeste, what's up? What's wrong?" I took a deep breath and sat on the pointy edge of the desk. "*Well*...I have something to tell you," I said with a crazy look on my face.

"It's a couple things," I stalled. Coia looked at me impatiently. I tried to get it out.

"I'm kinda messing with Keith Lawrence, and my period is late," I blurted out without meaning to so quickly. Coia sat down on top of her desk in shock and anger.

"Didn't we go through this in high school? Is this some strange déjà vu? *Girl*, you too old for this dumb shit," she nagged.

"I didn't come in here for a damn lecture. Plus the shit gets worse. My period is late. I don't know who the father could be, Keith or Kade," I said with a hint of embarrassment. "I don't know if I am for sure, but I have to figure this shit out," I retorted.

"You need your ass whooped, but since it's too late for all of that, we need to meet later and come up with a master plan," Coia suggested.

I was already the single parent of twins. There was no way I was about to have another baby. Not a damn chance!

"Okay, Sequoia, I will see you and the girls after work with lots of wine and a solution," I directed.

All night I avoided calls from Keith and texts from Kade. I did not want to say the wrong shit to either of them without knowing anything.

I left work and stopped by Walmart to get a pregnancy test. I walked past the pharmacy, got a pregnancy test, then I purchased bodywash and lotion to cover the test in my basket. I did not want to take a chance of someone seeing me buying a pregnancy test.

As I stood in line, the lady in front of me caught my eye. This lady was in a beautifully tailored navy blue suit with defined seams and gold buttons. Her black hair was neatly parted in the center and fell on her shoulders. She had on a medium-sized pearl necklace that pulled the outfit together and four-inch pump heel to match. She looked like a stylish lawyer. I had to give credit to a sister who had her shit together, and she did! She was on her phone while the cashier rang her up. I began to load my items onto the belt but did not want her or anyone else to see my pregnancy test. Why should I care what a stranger thinks of me? But, I was embarrassed for myself for making such stupid mistakes at my age. I placed the box carefully up on the conveyor belt and covered it with the bodywash and lotion by laying them on top. I looked down at my phone and saw that Keith had called and Kade texted me a few times. However this went down, if I was pregnant, Kade was the father biologically or not. I was gonna take this shit to the grave with me.

Abortion was the only answer. Kade may not have agreed with me, but he would have supported me. I could not answer them, not yet.

The cashier greeted me while I was putting my phone up. I looked down and saw that the stylish lady had left her wallet. She kept track of her phone, but not her wallet. I asked the cashier to quickly ring me up so that I could take the lady her wallet back.

I grabbed my flimsy gray bag and headed out of the door behind the lady. I started with a light jog and called out to her, "Ma'am, ma'am, you left your wallet." She was still on the phone and did not hear me. I chased her a little farther into the parking lot. She finally stopped at a two-door Mercedes AMG GT. It was smoke gray and gorgeous. She turned around, very puzzled. "Can I help you?" she said, slightly aggravated that I was following her.

"Ma'am, you left your wallet at the counter. I didn't want anyone to take it," I pleaded.

She instantly told the person on the phone, "I will call you back." She then extended her arm out for her wallet as I passed it to her.

"Thank you, young lady, for being so honest and giving my wallet. I was so busy on the phone, that I was just completely careless. I really appreciate you," she said sincerely. She asked my name. I told her, and she thanked me once more by name. Before she got into her car, she handed me her business card. Whatever her business was, I wanted a damn whip like that!

I returned to my car feeling like a hero. I had done a good deal for the day. I would want someone to do the same for me. For two minutes, I forgot about my problems.

UNWIND

As promised, we all met up at my place. The girls and I needed to unwind and just let some steam off. We all work at the same middle school. The four of us were overdue for some drinks, gossip, and food. We have been partners since college; Sequoia is the only exception. I have known her since middle school. Sequoia is the crazy, fun one with the same baby daddy problems that I have. It's crazy! We have so much in common. The both of us were engaged to brothers at the same time. We even became pregnant at the same time. Our kids would have been the exact same age. Nikki is the more level-headed one of the group. She is the oldest and more experienced friend. *Ding, dong.*

"Hey, Celeste, what's up, chic?" Nikki asked as she hugged me. I didn't get a chance to answer. "Did you know that Ms. Margret was fired last week? Girl, they told me she came to work drunk, had liquor in her cup, and fell asleep on the desk while the children were sitting right there," Nikki continued. Talking a hundred miles per minute, she was still halfway in foyer with this story. "So, I would not be a true Florida girl if I did not bring the jumbo garlic shrimp and snow crab legs," she boasted. We all screamed in excitement. It's a Florida thing, but garlic shrimp and snow crabs seasoned to perfection were a definite treat! As Nikki and Coia began to set up drinks and food, we waited for one last person. Jennifer was the last of the crew that makes us a whole. She was supersmart and resourceful. Jen makes boss moves at all times and moves in silence. We don't know what she has going on until after it happens. She makes big moves, period. Jen was also the late one. Just then, Jen arrived with sausage, corn, and eggs to go with the garlic crabs. We hugged and greeted one another. Jen was quiet and observant as usual. Coia and Nikki did all the talking, while I was looking crazy about my dilemma.

Coia, with her big, fat mouth, wasted no time. "Well, ladies, asked you guys to meet her because Celeste can't get her damn life together."

I interjected nonverbally by jumping up and closing the main hall door, making sure my girls were tucked away in their room before she said some ridiculous shit they did not need to hear.

Coia, partly drunk and partly being herself, explained, "Celeste is fucking with a married man and Kade and not using protection. She could be pregnant or have chlamydia, who knows."

There was dead silence in the room for, like, thirty whole seconds. That's a lot for this group. I felt I had to defend myself.

"I…well, he may be getting a divorce, and me and Kade are off and on, and I ain't got shit, no baby, no disease. Shut up, Coia," I said.

"I'm not the only person to do it, damn. I thought this was the no-judgment zone," I added. "Promise not to flip out if I tell you who," I said as I scanned the room. Well, of course, now their attention was really aroused.

Coia, with a sarcastic remark, said, "Nothing you say can shock me, bitch. I seen it all. Now spill it."

"Coia may be the only one who has a clue, but I have been messing around with Keith for about a year and a half now," I simply stated.

Nikki, with a perplexed look on her face, said, "Our principal. Bitch, are you crazy? The one who has a wife and three daughters?" she asked with seriousness.

"That would be the one," I responded. I felt like shit when she put it like that.

"That is a no-win situation. Husbands don't leave for the side chick no matter what his lying ass may tell you," Coia inserted her two cents.

"Fa real, I heard his wife was crazy. I don't know much about her except she's from New York or some shit. Anyway, he had to get her out of legal trouble because she did some crazy shit. I have to get the whole story. But after she got out of jail, they moved to Florida to start over. Just be careful," Nikki cautioned. She was right. They both were right. Keith was bad news for me. He was fine as fuck, but nothing good could happen from this shit. I was just flattered that I was the chosen one and attained certain benefits.

Then out of nowhere, the wise one took it all in and spoke, "You are a grown woman. It's your choice. You won't have all the answers tonight, so don't lose sleep about it. Just remember, you may be free to choose, but you are not free from the consequences," Jen offered as she sipped her pink moscato rose.

It got quiet once more.

Coia then dominated the conversation with one of her crazy-ass stories. "So y'all ready?" she asked. We were never ready for her crazy stories, but they were so interesting.

"Last week on my planning, I went with the social worker to do a home visit for Phillip Smalls in my homeroom. He missed, like, forty days this year. Failing every damn thang! Anyway, it was a typical hood, a typical day. When we pulled up in the driveway, I saw a muthafucking La-Z-Boy recliner on the front porch. I can't leave out the fact that the porch was raised. I knew it was gonna be some shit, ghetto shit! We pulled up. The social worker got out of the car, went on the porch, and knocked on the door. I stayed on the grass. Phillip's mama came out in a housecoat, bonnet, and some crazy shirt. She became indignant. His mama asked us why the hell we were at her house. The social worker handed her that truancy paperwork and shut all of that shit down. This wretched bitch sat her ass down on the recliner on the front porch to read the truancy report.

"She took her time to adjust herself in the recliner. She flopped down and kicked her legs up. Girl, she didn't have on a stitch of panties. You hear me? It was just a nasty, commando mess! All her damn cootie pop was out on the front porch. She was just swinging her legs like that, she had on joggers. Then the nasty ho took out a cigarette. She called Phillip out the house to light it. Phillip was looking crazy as hell, but he waved. His mama took a damn puff of the cigarette and set the damn truancy paper on fire. As the paper started to show flames, she said, 'Why the fuck y'all still standing in my yard? Bye!'

51

"Now, y'all know me, I normally curse a bitch out for that type of wretchedness, but I was on school time. I respected the raggedy bitch for standing her ground, but she went too far with the bullshit. I should have called Children Services. I mean that was not appropriate on any level, right?"

Nikki and Jennifer burst out laughing. They both had Phillip in their classes. Nikki then made it worse. "Girl, you saw Phillip's mama coochie? Is that what you just told me? You need a reality TV show, I swear," she commented, still laughing.

It was unanimous that we change the subject. I cut in with a different conversation.

"So in a couple of days, a few of the lead teachers are supposed to travel to Vegas along with the principal to go to a leadership conference on restorative practice for secondary schools. Any ideas on how this could benefit our school?" I asked. So Coia and Nikki alternated responses.

"Keep your legs closed… Use protection… Don't be a ho in public… Find another boo…," they said. Then Nikki got serious.

She looked more into the situation. "You know I don't ever get asked to those types of conferences," she implied. It did not take a genius to know why. Nikki will give her all from 8 to 4. She leaves the parking lot before the dismissal buses do. She is an excellent teacher, but she does not give any of her time for free. Do not ask for her time outside normal hours. You could get cursed out!

Coia cut in, "You can't go 'cause you ain't flashing no coochie or sleeping with the principal." I hate her ass sometimes! That's why I didn't want her to know about Keith.

Well, y'all, I went to the store and purchased a pregnancy test. I might as well take while I have my support around me.

The ladies had a few drinks and full bellies. I could handle the criticism because they were in great mood. However, it turned out their criticism came from a place of love.

Nikki yelled, "Go ahead, you might as well find out now so you can make some decisions!"

Coia asked, "Did you buy two tests? I might need to just check and see if I'm good. Shit, you never know."

So, I hesitated for a few minutes. I had thought out my options with Kade; I had not given Keith my thought. He was married. He had a wife and three daughters. Keith was not about to fuck that up for me or anyone else. I was not going to tell him if I was pregnant. I went into the restroom and sat down on the toilet. As I unwrapped the test, I prayed to God.

Please, God, get me out of this mess and I am going to do better. Lord, I know that I am a slave to the flesh. Help me do better, be better, Jesus. Amen! I peed on the stick and stuck it on the sink. Those two minutes of waiting were the longest damn two minutes in the world. I flipped it over. My face was stoic. I was in shock!

I forgot to even wash my hands. I flew out of the door and ran past everybody. I ran clean out of the front door screaming. I did two laps around my car, then headed back in the house. All three ladies met me at the door. They followed me with their eyes like I was insane.

Coia was confused as hell. "Bitch, what the fuck is wrong with you?" I was out of breath. I sat down at the doorway.

"I'm *not* pregnant, y'all," I celebrated. All the thinking and speculating was all for nothing. I will be using protection from this point on. But, I am not pregnant.

Coia's ridiculous ass ran around the car too, screaming and yelling, "Yes, bitch! Yes, bitch!"

We celebrated for the rest of the night.

TYPICAL NIGHT

It was a Thursday evening, and I just wanted to relax after work. I finally remembered to call my grandmother, but I couldn't talk long. My mama had aggravated me to death about calling her. I figured all Big Mama wanted to talk about was how to work her new fire stick. I thought my phone was sitting right beside me.

I searched my purse until all I could find was lint. I could not find my cell phone anywhere. "Mia, have you seen my phone?" I bellowed from the bedroom.

Of course, she brought her li'l pitiful-lookin' self in my room saying, "I think your phone dead, Mama. I didn't do it."

Of course, I countered her claim, "Yes, you did. Why in all of God's green earth do you have my flippin' phone, li'l girl?" I snatched it out of her little hands before she had a chance to answer me. I strategically reminded her they had a birthday coming up.

"I'm going back to do my homework now, Mommy, okay," Mia said dutifully, trying to get on my good side. She ran so fast her ponytails were bouncing, flying backward.

That shit ain't gonna work, I thought. I have to hide my cell phone from a six-year-old. I looked down and saw that my phone had a 3 percent charge. Just then, the phone rang. It was Keith. "Hello," I answered. It made me so excited to see his name across the screen of my phone. I was like a teenager.

"Hey, sexy. You packed everything that you need for the trip? It's in a couple days, and you know what I like," he bragged.

"Oh wow, it's that kind of conversation?" I asked.

"It can be," he responded right back. He had a peculiar laugh that signaled he wanted phone sex. I really had shit to do, but I was not going to disappoint him at all, especially before a big trip. I walked into the bathroom, which was the only place that I could be alone without the girls hassling me. I certainly didn't look the part but could sell it.

"So the next time I see you, I want it to be with your shirt off, jeans on and me zipping them down," I said as I got comfortable.

"Damn, tell me what you gone do once you unzip my jeans, babe," he requested.

"I plan on sitting you on the sofa and finish unfastening your pants. Once I have you 100 percent nude, I'm taking a taste test to get you hard. I'm not using hands either. I'm gonna start at the tip of the dick and work my tongue in circles like a corkscrew until I get just below the head," I described. By now he was stroking himself. I could hear him moaning on the phone, asking me not to stop.

"As I stroke you up and down with my mouth, I'm going to massage your…," I said, just about to finish when I heard him cum with a loud roar on the other end of the phone. That shit was so easy. It didn't take much. Keith switched the station quick once he reached completion. I was just about to ask him something about the trip when he hurried me off the phone. He was in an extreme hurry, or his wife came in the room, probably both.

I got nothing out of that quick little ordeal, but I was somewhat aroused. I did not feel like taking care of it myself, so I texted Kade to come see me. He knew exactly what that meant.

Just that quick, I forgot to call my Big Mama. I decided to call her the next day. I had to bathe the girls and feed them. I wanted them all situated by the time Kade got there. I had committed to help him with a deposition he was preparing for work.

Kade knew that I was about to travel out of town for business. I heard the alarm. Kade came in looking like he stepped out of a magazine. Lord, he was gorgeous. He came over in crisp white jeans and a loose-fitting polo jersey with a Gucci belt. He was adorable and sexy, six foot two of chocolate. He came up to me, gently grabbed my chin with two fingers for a kiss on my lips. I was captivated by the entire package. His cologne, Creed, put me under a spell. Kade was bringing out the big guns tonight. He reached out to hug me as if he had not seen me in months. His arms were strong and muscular. His touch, his look and smell were hypnotic. I turned around and saw three dozen roses on the table. Kade was so sweet. He settled in on the sofa. I cuddled next to him and rested my head in his lap. He watched Netflix with me for a little while until his fingers started to wander. Keith had huge hands but a very smooth touch. I saw where this was going. I got up to make sure that the girls were asleep. I didn't want to wake them.

I went back to the couch, removed my underwear. I put my index finger over my lips, motioning for him to be quiet. I opened the robe I was wearing to get him stimulated. I could see those nine and a half inches all the way through his pants. He could not hide that anaconda. I unzipped his pants, no foreplay this time around, and sat on top of him. I wanted him to feel my skin against his skin. Kade did not reject that idea. I was slipping and sliding all around his manhood.

"Put it in, babe, let me feel it," he begged. I raised my body up just enough to reach around for that inflated pole. It took more work than I thought. I finally got a good grip so that I could insert it inside me. It was large, so I had to sit down on it gently to open me up. Once I adjusted to the size, I was able to ride it with pleasure.

Every time we had sex or made love, my body had to adjust to his size. It was the biggest difference between Kade and Keith. Kade put both of his huge arms around my waist. I was facing him, looking right into those dark-brown eyes. He stared right back at me.

"Damn, Celeste, you are a beautiful woman, I love yo ass," he implored. I took the nonromantic approach.

"It ain't nothing like a beautiful woman riding your dick, is it, babe? You like this big ass sitting in your lap, don't you?" I teased.

That was the motivation that he needed to get off. I knew he was getting close because he was holding me so tight. I wanted to get up and let him cum on my breast, but he couldn't hold it anymore. Kade put a death grip on me and erupted inside me at the same time.

"Damn, Kade, I told you not to cum in me," I said softly.

"I could not help it, babe. You felt so damn good," he said apologetically. I got up leaking a complete mess. I went to get a wash towel for the both of us. We finished watching Netflix for the night and fell asleep on the sofa.

Kade woke up before me and decided to make us breakfast. I had no plans in going in to work today because I had to finish packing for my trip. My suitcase was on the love seat next to my window. Kade decided to attempt romantic gesture. He went to slide a card in my suitcase for me to find once I got to Vegas. I came in just in time to see him sliding it in. I tried to get his attention before he dug deeper in the suitcase and saw my skimpy underwear, seatless panties, and other matching bra sets.

"Hey, babe, I thought you were going to come in and enjoy breakfast with us girls," I said, tilting my head to the side for him to come with me. He dropped the card in the suitcase and followed me in the kitchen.

"Baby, I'm going to get the girls birthday presents next week. Those Disney princess bicycles are selling out fast. It's only a few months before their birthday. I can keep them in my garage until their party," Kade said.

I hugged him for being so sweet and loving my girls like he did. I still needed a ride.

"Kade, I may need you to drop me off at the airport, babe. Do you have court in the morning?" I inquired.

"That's a negative, babe, my first case is at 8:00 a.m.," he said. I hate it when he tells me no! I pouted like a two-year-old. I rolled my eyes at him and thought of my next option. Lord, I was going to have to get Coia to drop me off.

Kade and I seemed closer the past couple of weeks. *Maybe I will focus less on Keith and more on this relationship*, I thought.

I got the girls to school early. Ms. Nicholas was there in her usual spot waiting to see her students. Mia jumped out of the car onto the sidewalk to go hug her. I parked for a few minutes, which was against the rules, but I needed to speak to Ms. Nicholas quickly. I saw a note stapled to Mia's agenda requesting that we speak briefly. With my work hours and an upcoming trip, I thought this morning was a good opportunity to see her.

"Good morning, Ms. Nicholas, I just wanted to speak with you briefly about the note that you left for Mia," I said.

"Good morning, Ms. Belle. Yes, I was a little concerned that Mia seemed to be a bit aggressive with the other students, pushing, snatching things from them, and being a little mean to her classmates," Ms. Nicholas said with concern. As a teacher, I completely understood that this had to be addressed and she was obligated to say something.

"I will talk to her this evening when I pick her up, you won't have to worry about that anymore. However, I do teach her to defend herself if needed," I indicated.

The meeting was fairly short. We said our goodbyes. I hugged Nia and pulled Mia to the side. "Your li'l ass better not do anything today, not a push, whistle, or kick. Do you understand me? Or I will spank you with my belt and you can FORGET a birthday party, got it?" I warned her. Mia knew their birthday was in two months. She had been talking about a party constantly for the last three months.

I headed back to the car. I could not think of what happened that would cause Mia's behavior to change or to make her aggressive. Maybe I was spending so much time fulfilling my fantasies with Keith and Kade. I was not giving the girls enough attention. It did not help that I was headed to Vegas tomorrow.

When I get back, I am going to plan a family trip and develop an activity calendar just for us, I thought to myself. As a good parent, I had to share this information with Promise. Still sitting in the parking lot, I called. Of course, he did not pick up. So I left a voice mail. I was relieved that he did not answer. I did not want to hear his mouth that it was my fault that Mia was aggressive or that I was a slacking mother because I put my career before my girls. He had a thousand reasons why I was not Mother of the Year.

I had an appointment for my Brazilian wax. It was a feminine treat. Today I was getting the hair removal with jewelry. Coia's little sister explained the wonderful benefits of getting jewelry on her vajaja! According to her, it drove her boyfriend wild. The diamonds would only stay on a week, but I just needed it to last a few days. The jewelry would be a special touch for a special trip. I wasn't sure how that would work out with washing, but I was going to try it.

VEGAS

"Where the hell is Coia?" I said out loud. I was supposed to meet the group from work over forty-five minutes ago at the airport. This is exactly why I wanted Kade to take me. He was always punctual. Coia pulled up with the top down on her convertible BMW, blowing the horn loudly. She was extra late on such an important day. I put my luggage in the back of the car. I could not even hold it in. "What the hell took you so long, Coia? I could have called a damn Uber," I fussed.

She looked at me like I had really hurt her feelings, "Do you know what I been through?" she retorted.

Here we go! I was in for another one of her ridiculous-ass stories. Either way, I had to listen to it.

"Well, my mama called me about ten o'clock this morning and asked me to come take her to the store. You know my mama don't drive. So I told her I would be there soon, but I had to be quick because I was taking you to the airport. I put on my clothes and headed out the door. When I pulled up to her street, I saw a line of more than twelve police cars. I ain't never seen that many cops cars on the street. I pulled up by a Stop sign because the police were blocking the street to my mama's house. I was in instant panic. I thought somebody killed my mama, daddy, sister, somebody. I got out of my car and told the nearest police that my parents lived six houses down on the left, orange house. I showed him my ID, which still had their address on my license. You know I do all kinds of shady shit. I did not need anyone tracing a damn thang back to my address. Anyway, the police escorted me up to my parents' house. I was so uncomfortable passing by all of those cops. I just don't trust they ass. Their eyes were glued to me as I walked closer to the porch. The police knocked on the door. I was scared to death. Nobody told me anything about why so many police were there. My mama answered the door with a big-ass butcher knife in her hand. I was really freaked out then. The police motioned for me to go inside with Mama. He told us, 'No matter what, do not open the door and stay inside.' I ran and hugged Mama, thankful she was alive. We both armed ourselves with knives. I asked her if she knew what was going on. She said no, the police told her nothing. She was a nervous wreck, and Daddy was at work. Now you know they added that patio on the back of the house just off from the den. There is nothing but a wooden door that stands between the patio and the den. Mama insisted on going out onto the patio to get some ice out of the deep freezer. I didn't feel right about it. I begged her not to open that door. For once, she listened to me. We sat there maybe an hour, scared to do anything. Finally, I said, 'Mama, I can't leave you here alone. Let's just go.' She got her purse, and we went back to the front door. Policemen were out of their cars searching every yard on our street, including our yard. It seemed safe to go outside with three policemen in the yard. We motioned to one of the police that we were leaving while we locked the door. That's when we saw a big-ass police dog prowling through her yard, headed around the back of the house. One fine-ass officer escorted me and Mama back down the street to my car. I should have gotten his number. We made it to the car. As soon as we drove off, the neighbor Ms. Yvonne called and told us that the police found a man on Mama patio. He was hiding behind the deep freezer. The police dog had to drag him off of her patio by the leg. Now this is the kicker: the man had raped and killed an older lady three streets over from Mama's house the same day. He was hiding out on her patio, waiting for his next victim. If Mama had gone outside and got that ice, we would have been next. I probably would have fucked him up with that knife and cut his dick off. But, he could have hurt my damn mama."

I did not know what to say after that. "Oh my god, I'm so sorry, Coia. Are you okay? Is Ms. Edwards okay?" I asked.

"That's it, we are going to get our gun permits, and we taking our mamas with us. Shit is getting too wild in Miami," I added.

I felt terrible. That wasn't one of Coia's outlandish funny stories this time. It was a grim tale that could have ended horribly for Coia and her mama while I was mad about being late for a stupid trip. She seemed shaken up a bit. I was so relieved that nothing happened to either one of them. I could not imagine life without them.

"Coia dropped me off at the airport fifteen minutes before my flight. I felt really bad for being mad at her. I had fifteen minutes to get through security, check my bags, and find the other teachers. I saw the instructional coach along with the assistant principal, Mr. Smith, and two other teachers from the Science and Language Arts Department. Mr. Lawrence was at the ticket desk handling incidentals. He came over to give us all instructions for when we land. We exchanged phone numbers and discussed trivial issues. We heard "Flight 365 now boarding for Las Vegas." That was us! Everyone rushed for window seats, leaving me a middle seat right next to Keith. That was not my damn plan.

I was so scared to fly. I grabbed his hand and gripped it tightly. "I'm sorry, afraid to fly," I said.

"Don't worry, that's what I'm here for, to help you through this," he replied. His mouth said one thing, but the grip of his strong hand said something else.

We landed in a sunny, beautiful Vegas. I was amazed to see slot machines in the lobby of the airport. People were gambling before they even stepped on the soil of Vegas. Our group walked around like tourists watching in awe. Once we retrieved our bags, the excitement had set in that were in Sin City.

The landscaping was exquisite. The city spelled *enjoyment* with large signs of advertisements. I saw an ad on the side of a bus, "Two-for-one prostitutes," and MGM on the other side. The conference itself was directly on "the strip." Coincidentally, so was our hotel. It was massive. Giant floodlights were everywhere, even during the day. We wanted to settle in after a long trip. Part of the group checked in on one side of lobby, and the rest of us checked in on the other side.

It was clearly a conference; I saw multiple school groups that looked much like ours scurrying over the hotel lobby, trying to get room keys, exchanging phone numbers, and signing in for the restorative practice activities. In teacher language, that was not a party. They had meetings planned for us from 8:00 a.m. to 4:00 p.m. The trick was to divide and conquer. We had to be strategic about the meetings so that we did not die of boredom. We all wanted to go out and see Vegas, not be stuck in a hotel all day even if the hotel was striking. Keith picked who would attend the specific meetings. He did not want to make it obvious that we would be hanging out. He scheduled our meetings separately. He attended the morning session meetings with a smaller group, and I attended the afternoon sessions with my roommate.

My room was located on the fifteenth floor with Ms. Carmen, our instructional coach. I took my key out and swiped the card. We opened the door and were amazed at how large it was. It was an upscale extended stay with a full kitchen, living room, and two beds. I was late afternoon, and most of the group wanted to go to dinner. Getting to know Ms. Carmen was cool, people. We had never had the chance to sit and talk. As we unpacked, I learned about her husband and son. She learned about my twins, and we discussed being grossly underpaid as teachers.

It was getting late in the evening. Ms. Carmen decided to go down to the lobby early to take a chance at the slot machines. I told her that I would meet her downstairs when I showered. I called Kade to let him know that we had made it safely.

It was Vegas, and I was off the clock. I searched my suitcase and found my black slim fitting skirt with the high split. I coupled it with a red ruffle halter top that tied at the neck and dropped low at the breast. The blouse fit firmly around the waist and had no back. My hair was a straight jet-black twenty-two inches. It was flawless and laid. I searched my bag for my black shoes. I happened to find the card that Kade slipped in my bag. He left a love letter with $500 for me to enjoy myself. I loved him. I could not help myself.

I topped the outfit off with my tie-up black four-inch sandals. They were perfect for all ten white manicured toes. I was ready for Vegas!

I sprayed on my Burberry Britt and, with my purse in hand, headed for elevator. When I got off the elevator to meet the others, it was like being in a video in "slo mo"—all heads turned. I felt like a supermodel. So I strutted, slinging my hair from side to side. I enjoyed the spot light for that thirty seconds.

Ms. Carmen started it off. "Whoa, sexy mama, you transformed quickly," she said, a little tipsy.

Keith looked at me like he had never seen me before. His eye squinted, and his head tilted in my direction. Mr. Smith was a little drunk and did not hide his attraction. "Damn, Ms. Belle, you look edible. This is a big change from your professional attire. Right, Lawrence?" he said as he elicited a response from Keith.

After the shock of my homemade makeover, we all sat at a large table close to the bar. We ordered light refreshments instead of eating a heavy meal. As it got later, the Vegas nightlife became more inviting.

We linked up with a few teachers from other schools; they were two young women from Michigan public schools. One was a pretty Hispanic woman with large hips. The other was a woman with a light-brown complexion on the slim side who reminded me of T-Boz from TLC. They decided to go out with us to one of the clubs. We all came back to the table for "takers." I certainly was game for a night out. My roommate and Mr. Smith were a definite NO. They had a little too much to drink and were in for the night. Keith was down for going out. Of course, if I was going, he was going. It helped that three beautiful women were willing to escort him.

NIGHTLIFE

Breathing the night air invigorated me. The wind in the night sky blew through my twenty-two-inch weave and the split in my skirt. I should have really worn some other shoes. Four-inch heels were not a good look when walking down the Vegas strip. *Stunning* did not begin to describe the bright lights in Vegas. Everything there was a visual production. Even the traffic was astounding. In the walk, I was distracted by iridescent fountains, well-lit floodlights, kiosks, and crowds on the sidewalk. Our party of six decided to go to a club at the Venetian.

Colors of fuchsia and purple danced off the mirrored bar. Low lit lamps were posted on every column in the club for just enough lighting. This spot had booths, tables, and sofas. None were available because the place was packed.

As we entered the club, the guys motioned for us to walk ahead of them. We went through the security check. Keith and two other guys from another school came in behind us. Keith went to the bar with his two new principal friends. The Michigan teachers went to find us a table. I headed for the dance floor. The DJ was playing nothing but hits, and I felt like cutting up! I danced with a few people and saw that the ladies found us a nice table close to the dance floor. I went to have a seat and rest my feet; those shoes were killing me with all the walking and dancing. Keith came over with a drink for each of us. I thought that was very sweet. He sat beside me.

"I got your favorite Parrot Bay and pineapple juice," he said.

"Thank you, Keith, this is so sweet. I can't believe you remembered what I drink," I answered.

"You look great tonight, good enough to eat," he said while licking his lips.

I did not respond with words. I positioned myself closer to him and put my hand on his leg. If I had sat any closer to him, I would have been sitting in his lap. The ambiance was so chill. Keith gave me a sip of his drink. I winced with disgust, yuck! It was straight liquor, no chaser. He was in a great mood. We sat and laughed at different shit without a care in the world.

The music blasted into the halls of the Venetian. All of a sudden, the DJ played a throwback, Juvenile's "Back that Ass Up." I forgot that my feet had been hurting or that I was a little tired. I jumped to my feet and headed for the dance floor. I left Keith sitting right there. I didn't need any company. I took pride in dominating the dance floor solo.

As soon as the lyrics rang out, "Girl, you working with some ass...," I twerked like my life depended on it. Balancing going up and down in four-inch heels, I threw my ass in a circle and thrust my pelvis in rhythm. I turned around and shook these big hips, thick thighs, and small waist like a salt shaker. I rocked back and forth to the beat. The breakdown where Lil Wayne commands, "After you back it up then stop...then drop, drop, drop, drop it like it's hot," I went down as low as I could to the floor and twerked even harder—paused and twerked, paused and twerked again. I was hyped and did not want to sit down. The DJ played another favorite. This time, as I danced, Keith came to join me. He stood in back of me and began to grind on my ass with his hands on my hips. I could feel him gripping me tighter and grinding harder against my curves. I made it easy for him by poking my ass out. The music continued. Keith and I stayed on the floor. I saw Keith's friend come up and say something to him. The friend was an attractive guy. He looked like a professional football player. His entire body was muscular. He was about Keith's height. He was a handsome milk chocolate brown. His eyebrows were thick and dark. They complimented his skin tone so well. His eyelashes were especially long for a guy but framed his face perfectly. He had neat dreads that were twisted back with an immaculate tape up. Since he was also a principal, he had to keep that hair neat and clean. Keith's friend walked up and said something to him. They had a mutual exchange. To my surprise, he came up right in front of me. Keith was in back of me; the friend was in front of me. I was in the middle of a sexy-ass sandwich, and I loved every moment of it. After about thirty minutes of double trouble, we all went back to the table. The Michigan teachers had met a couple of guys and decided to head out. Keith, the other principal, one random guy, and I had the table to ourselves. A young Oriental chick walked over to our table and took the random guy by the hand to go with her. He must have known her or planned to get to know her.

It was just the three of us. It had to be about midnight. After hours of fun, Keith finally introduced the other principal as Dereck. I found that out on my own while on the dance floor. Dereck asked us both, "What y'all doing when you leave?"

My thought was, *To my room to get some damn sleep.*

"Shit, what you want to do?" Keith asked. I was mutual and planned to go with the flow. Dereck suggested we go back to his room because he had pure marijuana and Apple Crown Royal in his room. I did not smoke, but I was not going to be a party pooper either.

We decided to leave together. It was fairly short walk. I was so thankful for that. Dereck stayed in a hotel right next to our hotel. I was a little relieved; it minimized the chances of me running into a familiar face. My "ho" habits were a secret.

Dereck escorted us to his room. The setup was similar to our hotel room. It had a full kitchen, living room, and a single bed. We sat in the kitchen area. While they lit up and poured drinks, I excused myself and went to the restroom. I looked in the mirror. *Damn, I look a little rough*, I thought. My makeup was worn from the dancing and sweating. I did my best to touch up my face with my mini kit. Nothing changed about my outfit; it still fit like a glove. I popped gum in my mouth and walked back into the kitchen. The guys were laughing loud and enjoying their spirits while listening to Pandora on Keith's phone.

Dereck asked me if I was "good." He then went to the restroom. Keith then came close to me and hugged me.

"I have been enjoying your company. I can't wait to get these clothes off that sexy-ass body and make love to you," Keith said.

I responded by tongue-kissing him in the mouth. Keith started trying to unbutton my shirt.

"Keith, Dereck is in the next room. Wait until we get to our hotel, babe," I said with concern.

I brushed his hands down and looked at him crazy as hell.

Keith then hit me with, "Celeste, we are in Vegas, let's live a little. Check this out! My boy Dereck is very attracted to you. He just wants to watch."

I wasn't catching on. "Watch what?" I asked.

I tried to reason through this predicament; was he asking me if he could fuck me while Dereck watched? How well did he know Dereck? The thought never crossed my mind. I had never done anything like this before. I guess it couldn't do any harm if he watched.

Dereck came out the bathroom and sat down on the couch. Keith still had me in his grip and pulled me closer to him. I went along with it and kissed him back. He then let his hand travel into my blouse. My senses were heightened from being in a new environment with Keith and another fine guy watching.

"Keith, I need your shirt. Take it off," I requested. He unbuttoned it and gave it to me. I went to the restroom, found a washcloth, and ran warm water over it. I used Dereck's soap to lather up. I had to be careful not to know the diamond studs off my private part. It was sexy as fuck and expensive. In my mama's words, I took a ho bath. I ran the rag over my clit and instantly became roused. I removed all my clothes down to nothing. I used Keith's shirt as my cover. I walked out of the restroom with my entire front exposed from top to bottom. The diamond studs spelled out, "Fuck me right below my navel." Downstairs was good. My breasts stood up firm and plump. They peeked from underneath the shirt showing just a fraction of my cocoa-brown nipples. I was freshly shaved, no traces of hair. I bent over to shake my hair out, giving it that wild, sexy look. The curls fell over both sides of the shirt and onto my nude body.

I emerged from the bathroom and walked in the room slowly. Both jaws dropped to the ground. Dereck could not contain his excitement.

"Oh shit…damn, girl, you are fine as hell," he said while he grabbed his dick. "I ain't never seen no diamond pussy," he added.

Keith walked over to me, led me by the hand, and sat me on the bed. This was very new for me, but I liked it.

"Celeste, we are going to do all the shit we love to do to each other. The only difference is, we have a spectator," Keith whispered in my ear.

It was sexy yet informative. I whispered back, "Whatever you want, babe." I was eager to oblige. I slid to the edge of the bed directly across from Dereck, giving him a great view.

I gently pushed Keith on the floor in front of me. I wrapped one leg around his neck and folded the other so Dereck could see him eat my honeypot. "Be careful, don't swallow a diamond," I cautioned him.

Keith started with small kisses around my vagina. He then stuck his tongue out and licked slowly around my clit, never touching it. I moaned out loud, wanting direct stimulation. I looked over and saw that Dereck had removed his pants and shirt. His erect large joystick was sticking straight up through the opening of his boxers. It was humongous. Not only was it long, but it was thick. That shit turned me on to another level. I could at least fantasize that it was Dereck eating my center. Keith then went right into my spot with the tip of his tongue. He stopped, reached over to his cup sitting on the nightstand, and got a piece of ice. He put the ice on the tip of his tongue and circled around my clit repeatedly in a rhythmic pattern. I was getting close to my orgasm. Keith had both of my ass checks in his hands so he could pull my vagina closer to his mouth. He would stop and alternate licking me to sucking me. I kept my eye on Dereck while he stroked that big, long stick. I could not hold it anymore. I came loud enough for them both to enjoy it. Keith didn't want head. He turned and asked me to get on all fours, his favorite.

"Get up on your knees, babe, and face Dereck. I want him to see that pretty face," Keith demanded.

He wanted to enter me from behind. I did exactly as he requested. I arched my back and poked my ass out in Keith's direction. Dereck was in full jackoff mode. Keith got arrogant with Dereck and invited him in the conversation.

"Dereck, do you see this pretty ass she got? That was the best pussy I ever tasted," he told him. He inserted his dick in and was pounding me as he was talking. I had my legs spread from the back so that he could get in with ease. He gripped both sides of my hips, then he started playing in my damn hair. I was different. He rubbed it, moved it from my right shoulder to my left shoulder. He stroked it down my back as if he was styling it. I got into it. "Oh, you like that look, curly Spanish hair, don't you, Daddy?" I asked.

Keith stopped all of a sudden. He hopped off the bed and went to open the curtains. We could see the entire nightlife of Vegas from the window, which was more like an entire wall. The lights of every hotel combined bounced from the reflection of the window like a 4D picture. It was breathtaking. I was unfocused for a few seconds, taking it all in. Keith took a pillow to the window and pulled me over with him. Dereck wanted a piece of me so bad; I could see. I wanted him too. It was such a shame to let all that big stick go to waste.

Keith told me to get on my knees and put my stomach against the glass with my hands up. He stepped back and said to the both of us, "I don't know what's more beautiful, the Vegas view or your body."

Dereck had exploded ten minutes ago. He was back hard. He wanted more than a hand job. I wanted to feel him. Keith was great, but his size was small, could not compare to Dereck's. I needed the okay from both of them to engage.

Keith must have read my mind. "Dereck, what kind of friend would I be if I did not share my beautiful lady with you," he implied.

Dereck didn't hesitate for a second. He walked over and kindly asked me for consent to fuck the shit out of me. His body looked sculpted, truly athletic. Dereck did not spend time on the neck kissing. He came with a long, hard stick. His hands massaged my breasts as I knelt before the window. "I been waiting to touch you all night, gorgeous," he said. He got behind me, his large hands running across my nipples, while that long dick rested against my ass gave me a second wind.

"Can I ride it, Dereck?" I asked. He flipped me over so fast. With a large dick, I couldn't just jump on it like a horse. I had to work it inside. He and I moaned loudly at the same time. That anaconda reached erogenous zones I did not know existed. "Oooooh shit, I feel every inch of this dick," I moaned. I forgot Keith was right there watching. But he set this whole thing up. With that, I did not hold back. I was in froggy position, facing him. I eased down until I could feel his entire stick inside me. It was a tad bit painful because of the size, but I adjusted quickly. I never had an orgasm from penetration, never. Tonight I came all over his shaft. It was euphoric! Keith was on his third drink, rubbing his dick from the passenger's seat. I slowly got up because my legs were killing me. Dereck picked me up with muscles from the gods and sat me gently on the bed. Instead of inserting from the back like he had watched, he settled for missionary, sort of. I was fine with that. He raised both of my legs almost as far as they could go and entered me. I screamed loudly from pleasure and pain. Damn, he was a lot of man!

It was the wee hours of the morning before Keith and I returned to our hotel rooms. By the time we walked through the lobby doors, only the serious gamblers were out. I was exhausted from all the activity. We went to the elevator and headed our separate ways. He kissed me and said that he had the best time ever with me.

I got back to the room and was asleep for the next ten hours.

I had missed my conference sessions and my school meeting with the team. I hoped Keith covered for me. When I finally woke up, I looked at my phone and saw several messages from the twins, Coia, Keith, and surprisingly, Dereck. I must have been tipsy. When did I give Dereck my phone number? Out of curiosity, I wanted to call him back. Keith would probably feel some type of way, but who cares? He was married.

I got in the shower and got myself together. I worked up the courage to text Dereck.

C: Hey, what's up, handsome? Got your text.

70

He returned the text immediately.

> D: If you are not busy later, I want to see you again, with
> or without clothes. ☺

Apparently, I left a lasting impression on Dereck; he surely left one inside me.

I agreed to meet him without consulting or mentioning Keith. We met up early that afternoon so that I could at least attend our next team meeting.

I got to Dereck's room. He had fresh fruit laid out for me with orange juice and champagne. He also had an assortment of bagels and cream cheese. He was the romantic type.

"Wow, this looks exquisite. You didn't have to go through all of this trouble for me," I said. He was such a gentleman. I was genuinely impressed.

"Of course, I did. I wanted to have a real date this time, not a threesome."

We did this for the next three days. While Keith attended his a.m. meetings, I met with Dereck to cut down on confusion. I loved hanging out with him; the sex was phenomenal!

The trip had come to an end, and it was time to get back to reality. After the first outing, Keith and I were a little distant; he had to conduct business, and I was preoccupied with Dereck.

PICTURE DAY

Mia and Nia jumped all over my head while I tried to sleep. The time difference in Vegas had taken toll. Mia reminded me that she needed her hair fixed extra special today.

I sent her to get my phone, the comb, and grease. She brought the ribbons and hair bows on her own. She was funny. Nia was right behind her being such a sweetheart. She didn't care what I did to her hair just as long as it had bows in it.

"Mommy, I want to look pretty today at school," she said. I could not understand what the big deal was. Nia plopped in my lap and said, "We take pictures today at school."

They had on matching uniforms with ruffled baby blue and socks to match. Mia wanted to take a picture; this time, she asked for my phone. I showed her how to turn the camera around and aim it at herself. She squeezed the phone so hard that she actually took the picture and took a screenshot at the same time.

She loved the picture. I went to get dressed to take them to school. Mia decided she would take twenty more pictures of herself. It wasn't a problem because I would just erase eighteen of them later. She then went on the internet and started watching cartoons. She seemed pretty comfortable with the use of the phone.

They were so adorable, looking like mirrored images of baby dolls.

My mind drifted back to hanging out with Dereck in Vegas. I was crazy about Keith, but I really enjoyed Dereck. My phone rang.

I had forgotten that Mia even had my phone.

"Here, Mama." She handed me my phone without me asking.

I looked at the name of the caller. It was Keith. I could not talk to him in front of my girls. So I decided to call him back when I got home.

I had a little time and decided to walk the girls to class this morning instead of dropping them off in the parent loop. They skipped and hopped beside me as I held both of their hands walking across the street. We saw Ms. Nicholas.

"Good morning, Ms. Belle, it's great to see you," she said. I greeted her back. Nia went to her class that was a few doors down, and Mia went to sit at her desk beside a couple of classmates. I put my phone on silent so that I could talk with her quickly.

"How have things been going with Mia's behavior lately? Have you seen any improvement?" I asked.

Ms. Nicholas responded and explained that Mia had made much improvement. She was working and sharing nicely with her group. She had even become the classroom helper. She loved handing out worksheets and crayons.

I was so relieved that things had turned around. My absence for the past few days could have been a disaster. I'm glad Promise took care of them and gave the girls some consistency the past few days.

I was still exhausted and decided to go get back in the bed. I got undressed and hopped back into my plush covers. I sat my phone beside me so that I would not have to get up. There were several voice messages and text messages from Keith. What the fuck was going on? Did his wife find out about us, and was he trying to warn me? Maybe she was at the school to confront me, and I happened to be off today.

As I tried to put it together, I went through our messages. There was a string of profanity-laced messages. I took a closer look at what had been sent from my phone and saw a screenshot that Keith did NOT need to see. Mia mistakenly sent him a screenshot from my phone.

The messages between me and Dereck had accidentally been sent to Keith. I could have died. That's why Keith had been blowing my phone up. He wrote the most awful messages.

73

He called me a "lying bitch" and "stankin'-ass hoe"; I did not even know Keith spoke like that. I went back and saw that in one of the messages, I made reference to Keith's penis being small.

Wow, this was going to make work very awkward. Was he more upset that I fucked another guy behind his back or that I called his penis small? He set the whole thing up. I did not even know how I was going to face him again. How could he be so angry? He was married, WTF? How could he be mad at me?

It dawned on me that I had not called Kade since I had been back. A text message would be just effective.

"Come by after work. I miss you."

Kade did not deserve all this drama. But I was just too damn selfish to let him go. My mind was stuck on this Keith situation.

I reasoned it out. Keith is a professional; he would not let his feelings interfere with work.

I was fucked-to-the-up! Fatigue had settled in, and I sank into my bed. I fell into a deep sleep. After several hours of slumber, I woke up when I heard Coia's voice. She picked the girls up for me today.

They ran and jumped in my bed ready to tell me all about their day. I kissed and hugged them then sent them to their room. I needed to talk to Coia. I wanted to know if Keith had been acting different, angry, or out of sorts today.

Coia was in the kitchen heating up hot wings and macaroni and cheese. I sat down across from her.

"How was Vegas?" she asked.

I deliberated on telling her every single thing or part of the details. Coia is the least judgmental of all my friends. She just has a big mouth and would tell everybody. I would give her some information and see where this goes.

I told her about the scenery and the nightclub with other teachers. She figured out that Keith and I hooked up. That was a no-brainer. Then I moved the conversation to all the conferences that they offered.

"Bitch, all that shit you talking about is boring… Tell me more about the hookup part. Did you tell Keith that you thought you was pregnant, trick?" she reminded me.

With everything that happened, that seemed so long ago. I had forgotten about the pregnancy scare. I skimmed past all the juicy details and told her that we hooked up in his room a couple of times after late meetings.

"You have no enthusiasm when you tell a story. Your shit be boring as hell," she complained as she ate her wings.

I changed things up a bit. "Speaking of hookup, how was Keith today? Was he in a pretty good mood?" I asked.

Coia responded by saying that he was his same old self. The only thing that she could remember was that we got a new teacher this week while we were out of town. She started today. One of our teachers had gone out on early maternity leave, so we had a vacancy.

Coia went on and on with one of her stories. Her lips were moving, but my mind was preoccupied that I was going to face Keith with all this bullshit going on.

The next day, my nerves were frazzled. It was my first day returning to work since Vegas. I had to face Keith one day or another. I walked in the building as usual. Other teachers were walking in at the same time. It was a very normal day so far. The teacher's lounge was a madhouse as usual. I got the mail out of my box and talked with Nikki for a few minutes.

"Hey, I missed you, girl. Your second period was horrible while you were gone. You need to check them for that. I had to go over there and threaten them quite a few times," Nikki stated. The poor substitute teacher left early Friday. She could not take it.

It did not shock me that they misbehaved. "They are terrible when I'm there! I bribe them with candy and computer time," I said as Nikki and I both laughed.

As we both headed down the hall to our classrooms, I saw him, Keith. He headed out of his office that was close to the stairwell. He looked in my direction then turned away as if I did not exist.

I was slightly hurt, but it was to be expected. Four steps behind him, a new face appeared. She must have been the new teacher Sequoia told me about. She came out of his office right behind him, smiling. She was a very pretty lady with huge round eyes, more on the slim, athletic side. She was a fair-skinned lady with freckles. In a different light, you would think that she was white. Perhaps she was half white. Even so, she was an attractive woman. Her hair was shoulder length. It was a sandy brown, and it was her real hair! She had on the most confusing dress. It wrapped around her thin-framed body, then it just fell flat and jumbled at her knees. Very interesting look. Her shoes caught my eye. They were a platform heel, with a round toe. It resembled a golf shoe. It should have been a flat man's shoe. I guess her face made up for her horrible fashion choices.

Mr. Lawrence, the principal, formally known as Keith, walked in our direction with the new teacher. He walked up to Nikki, pretended I was not there, and introduced the new teacher, Ms. Snow.

"Ms. Snow, this is Mrs. Price. She's one of our best English teachers. This is Ms. Belle. She teaches social studies." He pointed to me without eye contact.

Ms. Snow greeted Nikki with a "Hello, how are you?" but took Mr. Lawrence's lead and did not address me at all. His goal was to make me look and feel small.

"Ladies, this is the beautiful Ms. Snow. She will be teaching science on the sixth-grade team. Please make her feel welcome," Keith said.

Did he just call her beautiful in my face, fa real? Why should I care; we aren't even on speaking terms. Nikki and I headed up to our rooms. "Well, that was interesting and a little disrespectful," she said snidely. I wanted to know her thought pattern.

"Why do you say that?" I asked with curiosity.

I knew what she meant. He practically flaunted the new teacher in my face. The last time I spoke with Nikki, she found out that I fucked Keith. This little stunt just made shit more difficult for me to explain.

Although the four of us hung out, Coia was the only one who knew most of my shenanigans. Nikki knew a portion; Jennifer knew even less than that. It's just how it was with a group of women friends. So I played Nikki's question off. "I don't know, shit, and I don't give a fuck," I said nonchalantly.

The day went by fairly slowly. I gave my second period the business for running the substitute away. They had to write the entire

Constitution for a test grade. I took it easy on a few of the students; we all know that in teaching, it's always five kids out of twenty-five that cause the major problems. Once we get those five under control, life is easy.

It was the final period of the day and also my planning period. I decided to go into the library to check out a class set of books for my students. I had a large cart of books for my class, headed to the library. So I had to use the elevator. I was three steps from the elevator, and I saw the new teacher Ms. Snow as already inside.

"Hold the elevator, please," I requested with my cart. This bitch looked me right in my face with a nasty smirk, turned her head, and pressed the button for the doors to close in my face.

THE SECRETARY

Ms. Gladys was a mean old secretary. Ms. Gladys was a cantankerous, bitter lady who looked down on others. She went to church three days out of the week but had little human compassion. That woman judged everybody. A parent once came in the front office in slides and a hair bonnet. Ms. Gladys scolded her for at least five solid minutes about proper dress when leaving the house. She did not bother to inquire that the parents' belongings were all burned down in a fire. In addition, when she found out, her focus was still on the parents' clothes and not the tragedy. She may not have killed anyone, but I know she ran over a puppy or two. There is just no way to get on her good side. She was Krampus to the kids and a boogeyman to teachers.

I tried the "Hi, Ms. Gladys, you look very nice today!" All that she gave me was a grunt and an eye roll.

Ms. Gladys always tried her hardest to keep me away from the principal—ridiculous. It was like she knew something. If I went in on my planning and I needed to see Keith, she would walk her happy hips from around her desk and say with a manly voice, "He in a meeting right now with the deputy superintendent." It was hard to believe that he was in a meeting twice a day, five days a week. So I had to be strategic and outsmart Ms. Gladys if I wanted to see Keith during work hours.

It was crazy because Ms. Gladys's niece is in my class—third-period class. I don't hold it against her that her aunt is Satan in a dress, evil ass! Between Ms. Gladys and Ms. Jackson, I may have to poison one of their old asses just to survive life. It was too much. I had one at work and one at home.

I wanted to clear the air. I had to talk to Keith face-to-face, like adults. I had to play her game. She took pleasure in tragedy and sad stories. I pretended that I had a dire emergency. "Ms. Gladys, please excuse me for coming in unannounced. I'm so upset, I may be out for a week or so because I have a serious tumor," I said with fake sniffles. She did not like me, or anyone for that matter, but she was so nosy she could not help herself.

"Ooh, girl, I knew you didn't look right, just been looking a mess lately. You just need to pray 'bout it," she advised. "I guess I can let you in for a few seconds."

"When they plan on taking the tumor out?" she asked. Ms. Gladys walked over to his door and peeked inside to let Mr. Lawrence know that I was waiting outside to see him. As soon as Ms. Gladys sat down, I looked up and saw this elevator bitch again. Ms. Snow emerged from Keith's office in her terrible-fitting dress and grandma shoes. Her hair was plain but pretty. She was a very pretty lady; she just did not have any style. She was just a skinny, pretty lady. I thought Keith liked more pizzazz in a woman, not plain Jane. I'm not a man; what the hell do I know?

She sauntered out of the office as if she had clout over us all. She had a briefcase on her shoulder and a writing pad in her hands. She came out laughing and giggling at whatever Keith had just told her. She looked over in my direction, snickered, and rolled her eyes. Ms. Gladys watched her walk out and said to no one in particular, "I don't know if I like her. She is too clingy to Mr. Lawrence."

For once, I agreed with Ms. Gladys. I had done nothing to this bitch, nothing! I was out of town. Someone must have told her something awful about me for her to act this way. It was either his bitch ass or one of these jealous old hags. She walked past me and out of the office. Keith came to the door and followed her out of the office with his eyes.

He then turned to me in disgust. The look on his face was like "What the fuck are you doing in my office?"

He called me in, "Ms. Belle."

I walked in quickly just to get the awkwardness over with.

"Mr. Lawrence, Keith, uuhm, I'm so sorry that things escalated to this point. I understand that things are over. I just want us to have a good working relationship," I implored.

He looked me in the eyes and responded, "So you thought it was a good idea to call my wife and tell her that I was having an affair?" he asked furiously. I looked completely perplexed. Call his wife? That's not even my style. Why would I do some dumb shit like that and implicate myself?

"That shit didn't work. Your plan blew up in your face. I don't care what you do. My wife is at home with my three daughters. They are the only women that I care about. Now what can I help you with?" he said coldly.

That shit hurt. I was low-key devastated. There was no other way to put it. I would never ever call his wife. That would be really stupid. Someone called his wife, but it was not me. I didn't know how this was going to work, but I was contracted until the end of the school year. I would try to avoid him as much as possible. I left feeling stupid for going in there at all.

I walked to the parking lot and caught up with Coia and Nikki. "Hey, y'all, we need to get our tickets for Jazz in the Gardens. It's going to be sold out soon," Nikki said. I was a little zoned out, but I needed that distraction. We had to decide if we were going in our girl group or taking dates.

"When are you gonna tell us what happened with Lawrence?" they both asked at the same time.

"The weekend, I will fill you all in, promise. I gotta go get the girls," I said, leaving in a hurry.

I called Kade as soon as I got inside the car. I needed a familiar, comfortable companion to talk to. Kade picked up on the first ring. "What's up, baby girl? You have been a stranger lately," Kade said. I felt awful. I cheated on him in Vegas and hadn't called him in three days. I told him I just wanted a quiet night in with him. He agreed that we needed it.

I picked the girls up and started a pot of spaghetti. It was quick and easy. The girls loved it. Kade walked in and hugged the girls. I had to be either blind or crazy. Kade was fine as hell. He reminded me of a much-taller Dereck, maybe just a little darker. But that athletic body was unstoppable. His muscles seemed to have grown in the seven or eight days we were apart. Mia was on his left arm, and

Nia was on his right arm. They jumped all over him. It had been a while since he had seen them too. He brought Barbie dolls for the both of them. He's so sweet! I'm so stupid for gambling with such a good man. He went in my room and changed into something more comfortable so he could eat spaghetti and watch TV with me. We didn't have sex. We were like an old couple. After dinner, Kade did the dishes while I bathed the girls and got them ready for bed.

He joined me in the room and helped me pick out a conservative suit for our deputy-superintendent visit. I let him pick out everything like he was the doting husband.

He found an ankle-length red skirt. "How is this, babe?" he asked me. Where in the hell did he find that conservative atrocity? I hate the color red. I don't where red at ALL! That had to be Coia's or Nikki's dress hanging in my closet.

"Kade, you are trippin'," I said.

"Okay, I found something else. I think this pink skirt would be nice with a shirt. That's the best I can do, babe," he said laughing. I thought it was actually a good idea to wear the fuchsia pleated skirt with a nice silk blouse—light pink, that's it. I found the perfect pair of shoes, and I had an outfit. I laid out the perfect pearl necklace and matching earrings.

We cuddled and laughed while comparing our lives to Martin and Gina. I loved him.

We sat in bed watching old episodes of *The Fresh Prince vs. Martin*.

My lesson plans were finished, outfit ready, and I felt good for the first time today.

The phone rang. It was my mom, but it was late and I did not feel much like talking. The conversation was quick. "Hey, Ma," I said.

"Hey, CC, I was checking to make sure you made it back from Vegas. I haven't talked to you in a couple days, girl. You sound tired, you better get you some rest. You know, your grandmother has been trying to reach you. Make sure you call her. I'm tired of telling you that. And, don't go another three days without calling me again, understand?" my mom scolded.

"Yes, ma'am," I responded, promising that I would call her back tomorrow.

GHOSTS FROM THE PAST

Although Keith and I were not speaking, he couldn't help but notice that I looked like a freshly pricked rose in my fuchsia and silk that Kade picked out for me. I had to give myself credit. I was striking today with my makeup and hair on point. He saw me walking down the hall, and he could not help but look at me as I sashayed in my three-and-a-half-inch heels. I was getting my stride back. Ms. Snow happened to be standing close to the entrance along with several other teachers and saw me from a distance. His jaw dropped to the floor, and her red complexion turned green with envy. She stared at me harder than Keith. I knew I was extra cute; she looked plain as usual.

I headed to my class feeling delightful. I made sure that my lesson plans were out and available. I had all my copies made, and the outline of my board configuration was done.

I conducted first period as usual. I was prepared no matter what period they came in. We worked on a lesson about "rewriting history." The students were writing essays about major milestones in their lives. I was on the board, modeling how to start the thesis when I saw a tribe of unfamiliar guests come into my room. I continued writing as if no one was in the room but me and my students. One of my students, Patrick, raised his hand to share his ideas. It started a chain reaction in the room. Patrick's idea triggered two other students' responses. Their dialogue invited the other students in the discussion. The entire class was engaged. I saw a few of the visitors nod their heads in agreement like they were impressed that my students were savvy like that. A couple of the guests spoke with my students. Others looked around my room for evidence of student work and grading rubrics. Keith was the only asshole looking for something negative. I saw him thumb through my lesson-plan book as I circulated to help students. My plans were in order, thank God. He still wrote notes in his li'l raggedy-ass notebook.

The visitors stayed for about twenty minutes then exited. As they left, I could hear Keith say, "That was nothing compared to what you will see in our new science teacher's room."

Fuck him. I know my kids did their thing! He was just being petty and vengeful. I did not like his ass at all. One of my students had her head hung down low. It was Destiny, my baby doll. Destiny had transferred from my last period to my first-period class. I walked up to her to ask what was wrong. She had a tear running down her face. I felt bad; I wasn't sure what was wrong. While the other students continued their discussion, I pulled Destiny into my office. I was able to speak to her and monitor the rest of the class with the door open. I hugged her. "Destiny, whatever it is, I'm sure it will be okay, pumpkin. You can talk to me," I said to her in a gentle manner. She handed me her essay. She could not say it, but she had written about it. As I began to read her essay, it became clear that her stepfather had been abusing her for a couple of years. He started out touching her when she was in elementary school, then he moved to raping her while her brother was in the next bed. According to her essay, her mom did not believe her. I did not know what to say to her initially. She was so broken and dejected. I just hugged her and let her know that we (the school) were going to get her some help. Her hair was all over the place from me holding her while she cried. I wiped her face with a tissue. All teachers are mandated reporters. It was not my job to conduct the investigation. It was my job to report suspected abuse. I walked over to my phone and called for Mr. Smith, the assistant principal. It took him all of five minutes for him to get to my classroom. Mr. Smith walked in. "The superintendent was very impressed with your students today. Congratulations," he said. Too much was going on for me to elaborate on what the superintendent said. Mr. Smith saw that something serious was going on. I explained the situation with the essay. Mr. Smith agreed to watch my class while I reported the allegation to Child Services. Destiny looked so sad. Her face was red from crying. I wished that I could take her home with me.

I made the call downstairs in the nurse's office so no one would hear me. Sitting at the nurse's desk in the empty office, I felt a sick feeling come over me. There were pamphlets all over the office about rape. That was when it hit me! I had a horrible flashback.

I was nineteen years old in the best shape ever, looking better than most (in my mind) and invincible. The most popular fraternity was throwing the "livest" party ever in the University Center. I had been studying hard for finals and had neglected my hair. My good friend Sandra knew all the best stylists in town. She told me the best place to go, which was in the hood, but I was okay with that. What she did not warn me about is the parking situation. There was nowhere to park. They were always crowded because they had the best beauticians in Miami, hands down! The building was off a main thoroughfare adjacent to a community park. It wasn't it the best part of town, but it wasn't worst. Either way, I had a party to go to tomorrow: I had to get my hair slayed.

The beautician had to work me in, so I was waiting a very long time. The entire time I thought, *Damn, I gotta learn how to do my own damn hair.* She finished my hair, and I loved it! "It's dark out there," the owner said. I did not realize that it was so late…1:00 a.m. Damn, no wonder I was exhausted. I would have to sleep sitting up. It was a side ponytail with forward spikes and a swoop that went across my forehead.

I grabbed my Dooney bag, gave my hair another once-over, and headed out the back of the salon. The beautician stopped me before I walked out of the door and said, "I only have one more perm to do. If you wait a few minutes, we can walk out together. I had a little walk to go. I was parked in an alley located in back of the shop. It was very dark with a dim light that hovered over my little black sports car. Looking down for my keys like a dumb ass, I did not see the three men approaching me from my right side. My heart raced; fear ran through me like never before. The men were walking rapidly. With any luck, I was thinking someone else would walk out of the shop…or a car would turn the dark corner and shine its lights in my direction. No such luck occurred. So, I had to pray that these men were upstanding citizens! The men walked past me rapidly, and I was so relieved I heard the taller one say to the bum with a yellow striped shirt, "That bitch fine as hell." I was not about to say a word to bring any more attention to myself. I heard them all let out a sinister chuckle in unison. It wasn't until they circled back around that I realized something was happening. They recognized a sadistic opportunity was before them. One was a taller thin dude with a scruffy beard and filthy nails. He looked dirty, and his clothes smelled like he had them on for days. Another one had on the yellow stripped shirt. He was the short muscular type. He was a little cleaner but mean with awful teeth. He seemed to be the ringleader. The last one was on the smaller side and seemed detached from the situation. He was trying to get home. They walked up to me and surrounded me. I thought they wanted my purse or money.

"You look pretty tonight, Ms. Lady. It must be fate, us meeting like this," the ringleader said.

I looked around for help from anyone. Only three the hard way were there. "I have to get to my car," I said to all of them. The ringleader grabbed my arm and yanked me near a dumpster in the alley. There was cardboard on the ground. He tossed me on top of it. I landed roughly on my stomach and attempted to scream. The tall guy dashed over to me and covered my mouth. He was filthy and smelly. He shifted me where he held both of my arms. I wrestled to get loose. It was no use. The ringleader dived on top of me and ripped my underwear. That disgusting pig took his grotesque penis out and shoved it inside me. I screamed in pain, then he covered my mouth again. I bit his hand. He then slapped me across the face. When he was done, he got up and started to switch over with the tall nasty guy. I had a small window of opportunity to escape with my life. They weren't going to just let me go. They planned on killing me in that alley. The third guy was in shock that all this was taking place.

"I got a daughter that age, man, this is fucked up," he said. A barking dog in a nearby yard saved me.

He must have heard all the commotion. There was a sharp object; it was like a broken umbrella stem. I managed to reach for it with my left arm. When the ringleader got up, I kicked him as hard as I could. The tall guy was coming around for his turn; I stabbed him with umbrella stem in his stomach. They both yelled loudly. "This motherfucking bitch just stabbed me!" he screamed.

I yelled, "Help, help, rape!" as many times as I could.

The dog's owner came out to the gate. "Who's out there?" he yelled. All three guys took off running. When I saw that they were gone, I picked myself up off the ground. I ran to my car as quickly as I could and got in, crying uncontrollably while throbbing in pain. I locked the doors and drove out of that alley. I was devastated. I had blood dripping down my legs and my face from being hit. My fingers touched the blood; it was bright red. I fucking hated the color red after that. It smells and looks like blood! I still hate the color red.

After the flashback, I gave Child Services all the information and provided all the required information for the investigation. I had not eaten all day. I felt a little weak. I think it was due to the horrid memory of being raped. I was nauseated. The women's restroom was housed in the nurse office, so I was in luck. I let all my hurt and anger spew out in the toilet, over and over again. As I was coming out, I saw Ms. Snow come into the nurse's office. Oh god, not her, not now! I was not in the mood for her bullshit. She could see the look on my face that I was not myself. I was too sick and weak to defend myself. The room swirled around me; colors of red, orange, and yellow circled around the room. I saw a dash of white and suddenly fell unconscious on the hard tile floor. In what seemed like an hour, blurry visions of the school nurse, Mr. Lawrence, Sequoia, and two other teachers surrounded me.

"What happened?" I asked in a raspy voice.

"We found you unconscious in here on the floor all alone. We don't know how long you were out, but we have to get you to the hospital. Your blood sugar was extremely low," the nurse responded.

The crazy thing about trauma, you never know who or what will trigger traumatic events.

The emergency medical techs pushed me out into the hallway, with Coia holding my hand.

"I got the girls. I will call your mom and meet you at the hospital," she said nervously. As I was carted off, I caught a glimpse of Snow. She had a sinister smile as if she had accomplished something great. Then I faded out once more.

NEW SHERIFF

Those three days in the hospital were the longest days ever. I was so concerned about my babies at home and school. Doctors diagnosed me with diabetes. That was so strange since I had never had any symptoms. I was pregnant with twins and did not even experience gestational diabetes.

Sequoia, Nikki, and Jennifer came over to make sure I was okay.

"Girl, you scared the shit out of us. You just fainted in the middle of the day on the floor. The nurse said it looked like you had been there for at least twenty minutes," she explained.

I thought that was strange because Snow was right there when it happened. She just left me there?

"Bitch, you are too young to die from diabetes. Get your damn life together," Coia said coldly.

Nikki surveyed the house and started cleaning and straightening up things like she always did.

"I supplied your substitute teacher with emergency lesson plans so that Lawrence would not have a word to say about your classes being covered. If it's worth anything, he did seem concerned about you," Nikki added.

The topic changed to my least favorite person.

"Did you know that Lawrence made Snow the department chair for science?" Coia agitatedly stated.

We were not a bit surprised, but she was so unqualified for the job.

"My friend in Human Resources said Snow had not even passed her professional certification. I even heard that she had to take the math section of the general knowledge exam three times before she passed it. Now she is supposed to head what department, the one for idiots," Coia chimed in. If five idiots from five different villages formed their own village of idiots, she would be the village idiot of THAT village. That's just how I felt.

This was always the complaint of authoritative figures in these positions. They hired based on who they liked, not who was qualified.

I finally joined the conversation, "Keith ain't shit, you know that. He makes decisions based on his limp-ass penis, not talent or skill." None of us were intimidated by Snow's li'l power; we would go about our business as usual.

Someone knocked on the door as we were talking. Jennifer went over to the door so that I would not have to get up.

"It's Kade," she said to all of us.

He walked in with groceries in both hands. Kade set them on the counter, greeted all my guests, then leaned over and kissed my forehead.

"I'm cooking lasagna. You ladies staying for dinner?" he asked.

We finished up early because we all had to go to work the next day and rehash all this crap "up close and personal." They all walked to the door at the same time. "No thanks, Kade, we have an early day tomorrow," they said in unison as if rehearsed. Nikki pulled me to the side as she walked out. "Kade is a good man. Don't fuck this up."

It was a sunny blue morning. I looked forward to heading back to work. My students missed me, and I missed them the same. I walked into my first-period class, and they all had a huge sign that read, "Get better, Ms. Belle, we love you!" It was the sweetest thing ever. I was so proud of my kids when I saw all the mounds of work that they had done while I was gone. They actually did work. As the students worked in groups, I checked my email. I hate after-school meetings on the fly; they are such a waste of time. Whatever it is could probably be said in an email or newsletter. This time the email said that the meeting was voluntary. *Voluntary* usually meant he was going to do some shady shit and did not want anyone questioning him. He called the meeting out of obligation to the union contract.

I wanted to thank the nurse for her concern and help, so I went down right after I escorted my third period to lunch. Mrs. Thatcher was a middle-aged lady, very sweet. She cared about the students and the staff. She always wore her white hat, coat, and scrubs dutifully. Although she was a heavy lady, she was still a very nice-looking lady with a great spirit to match. The most memorable thing about her were her Crocs. She had blue Crocs with all kinds of patches on them. It was a hoot for the students. They loved her Croc patches.

Nurse Thatcher was in her office. I walked in unannounced. She was so delighted to see me she did not hide her emotion. "I'm so glad you are okay and back with us. I was worried about you, Ms. Belle," she indicated.

"Thank you very for your concern. The doctors in the hospital told me I have diabetes. Of course, you know that it can be managed if I take proper care," I clarified. I hugged her because she was such a sweetheart and thanked her again.

"You have to monitor your sugar levels throughout the day. I have plenty of juice and crackers, whatever you need to get through," she inserted with concern.

"I have one question, Nurse Thatcher. When you found me on the floor, was anyone in here with me, or did anyone alert you that I was in here?" I asked.

"No, I found you unconscious on the floor and called rescue," she answered.

I headed back to pick up my class and decided to stop by the Student Resource Office. Our school officer was a lazy man who did very little to secure our campus. He barely broke up fights. I knew it was a slim chance that he would help me, but I had to try.

I knocked on the door. I could hear music blaring from his desk speakers. He turned it down as soon as I sat in a chair. I asked if he could bring up footage from the day I fainted in the nurses' office. I just wanted to make sure that I was not crazy. He took his time answering. "How are you, Ms. Belle? I heard that you took a spill. Let me see what I can do," he replied. I guess sympathy paid off. He started typing on his computer for a few minutes and lowered his music to a silence. The officer motioned for me to come around the desk so that I could see the computer.

"Okay, so this is the day that you fainted. This is you coming out of the restroom, Ms. Snow was there, and it appears that you fell on the ground," he observed. I watched closely as Snow looked at me on the ground, walked over to the sink to wash out her coffee cup, and looked at me again before walking out.

The officer seemed concerned that Ms. Snow wasn't alarmed when I fell on the ground, nor did she run out in a rush to get me help. "That's strange, Ms. Snow just washed her coffee cup and walked out," he confirmed.

"Can you tell how long I was there on the ground before someone found me?" I asked.

The officer marked the time on a sticky note and fast-forwarded the cameras before he answered. "You were there unconscious thirteen minutes before Nurse Thatcher came in and found you on the floor," he stated.

That was all that I needed. That malevolent bitch left me there to die. She didn't even try to get me any help. No matter her personal feelings, that was dead wrong. I was *so* fucking upset.

I had two more classes to go. It was important not to take my anger out on the kids or to do anything irrational. The last thing I felt like was a faculty meeting, again. I wanted to run straight to Keith and tell him what that wretched degenerate had done, but he probably wouldn't believe me.

It was the last period of the day, and I met Sequoia and Nikki in the hallway. We agreed that we would go to the meeting together. There were only eight other teachers there. He told us all at the last minute. Of course, Ms. Snow was there floating around Mr. Lawrence like a pesky mosquito.

We sat down close to the rear of the media center. Mr. Lawrence started the meeting promptly.

"Good afternoon, everyone. I'm grateful to those who were able to attend this meeting last minute. I wanted to make you all aware of some of the new changes that may impact your positions. First, I want to welcome our newest member to the team, Ms. Snow. Please stand up and wave," his lame ass said.

Coia, Nikki, and I all were looking crazy; why the fuck was this important? We were waiting for the other shoe to drop. "I know he didn't call a meeting to showboat this basic bitch," Coia complained. I was still very angry with her for leaving me unconscious on the floor. I decided not to share that with my friends at the moment so that there would not be an after-school fight.

Mr. Lawrence continued going on about nothing.

"As you know, our school will be the pilot for a new science program. Ms. Snow, with her innovative teaching and great skills, will be the head of that program. It comes with a hefty stipend. If you are interested in signing up, please see her after the meeting. Also, she will be taking over the after-school program. There are still a few openings in the after-school tutoring programs. You can also sign up for that today," he said with encouragement.

"Wait, that after-school program was mine. I was in charge of that," I reacted.

Coia and Nikki both stated at the same time, "He is so damn shady." Keith did not have a conversation with me as a professional. He just yanked the job from under me and gave it to Snow. We did not even stay to hear the rest of the meeting. The three of us walked out together.

We were equally pissed about Mr. Lawrence's immature behavior.

"That motherfucker is horrible. He is vindictive and heartless," Coia said as we got to the hallway.

All I could say is, "I detest his punk ass. He is more a bitch than any girl that I know."

Coia suddenly remembered that she was supposed to pick up her check from the bookkeeper before she left school today. Actually we all were supposed to pick up money from the bookkeeper. With the hospital and Keith stupid shit, I had forgotten.

"Thank God, she's still here," Nikki said aloud.

Sequoia walked into her office first. Nikki and I filed behind her.

"Hey, you ladies caught me right before I was about to leave. Ms. Edwards, I have two checks for you. Mrs. Price, I have one for you. Ms. Belle, I don't see your checks. I believe the new after-school supervisor, Ms. Snow, put your checks in your mailbox," she said.

The bookkeeper exited the office with us standing there, looking crazy. I did not waste time. Immediately I checked my mailbox and did not see any of my three checks. I don't know what the fuck the bookkeeper was thinking to release my checks to her. I would deal her tomorrow. "This shit is getting out of hand," Coia said to no one in particular.

The crew walked with me back down to the media center because this was unacceptable. Ms. Snow was still buzzing around Mr. Lawrence.

"I just came from the bookkeeper's office. She said that you had my checks and were supposed to put them in my mailbox," I accused Snow.

"I don't know what you are talking about. I would not have a reason to have your checks. This is inappropriate," she whined.

"Mr. Lawrence, I just left the bookkeeper's office. All three of us heard the same thing, that she gave the checks to Ms. Snow and that she was going to put them in my mailbox," I stated with no patience.

"I'm sure it will turn up somewhere. There is no need to get all wound up. We will take a look at it tomorrow, right, Ms. Snow?" he alleged.

I was beyond upset. I marched to my car and just yelled as loudly as I could. It's one thing to be petty, but it's another thing to fuck with my money. I called Kade from the car.

"What's up, baby?" he said as he answered the phone. My conversation unraveled like a spool of thread. I explained to him about the day that I had with my three checks and finding out that Snow left me in the nurse's office unconscious. I had to be careful not to reveal that we had a bitter love triangle that's ending badly. Kade could not know that I cheated on him with Keith.

TWO AT A TIME

The bookkeeper was just as concerned as I was that I did not get my "per diem" money from Vegas or my two after-school checks. She found me in the hallway that morning.

"Ms. Belle, I did the research, and Ms. Snow had your checks and three other people's checks. She assured me that she would make sure that you all got them. I was rushing and did not double-check behind her. No worries, if they don't turn up today, I will reissue them and give them to you personally," she said apologetically.

I felt better about that part. The question was, what did that trick whore with my money? I could officially say she was really trying to fuck with me.

After speaking with the bookkeeper, I had calmed down tremendously. I was cleaning up the mess my previous class made. The students had just transitioned to their third-period class, and I was looking forward to a quiet planning period. With red pen in hand, I was correcting essays. I was trying to get prepared for the next day. Suddenly, my door opened abruptly, almost knocking over the wastebasket behind it. Live in the flesh, the wicked witches of the East and West entered my room with evil smirks on their old wrinkled-ass faces. The fact that two teachers walked in *my* class like they owned the placed almost made me lose it!

"Ms. Belle, we need to talk to you," the first hag said as she quickly scanned my room. She looked like Respusia from the movie *Norbit* (the scene when she took her wig off.) I looked around to make sure they both were talking to the right person. The other old bag was standing there, looking like a throwback Diana Ross with that ridiculous red weave all over her head. Ms. Taylor/Respusia then proceeded to say, "One of the teachers told me that you have a problem with the way that I'm teaching one of your students in my after-school program. Actually they said you wanted me replaced with your friend, Ms. Edwards. I don't answer to you, just know that. And, by the way, Ms. Snow is my niece. I don't want no problems with you confronting her."

Why did Satan tempt me so much? I had to straighten the damn "old school twins" before I end up in jail. So without even thinking, I stood up mystified, angry, and eager all at the same time. I had **that** talk in my head before words escaped my lips. I could lose my fucking job today on some absolute foolishness. Before I let go of both of these bitches, I had to think about the consequences. What if another staff member walks in during this exchange? What if the principal decides he wants to see me at this hour, in this moment?

Oh well… All rational thoughts absconded in this moment, right now!

"Let's start with you just so that there is no confusion, Ms. Taylor, Big Mama, whatever you prefer to be called. Don't you ever in all of your 68 years and 482 lb. of life come in my class thinking you run a damn thing, because I got time today!

"I don't give a frog's fat fanny if the first lady of the United States was your niece. Don't come to my classroom challenging me like we are on the streets. This is a place of work, but since you took it there, know this: if I had a problem with you or your teaching, I would come straight to you. Unfortunately, you will never understand new-age teaching because you sit at your desk and teach from a chair. You give out hands calling it 'teaching.' You can train a dog to hand out papers. And you get a check for it?" She tried to interrupt me; I just got louder, drowning out the sound of her voice.

"The biggest mistake you ever made was coming into my classroom like you were some old lady gangster crew telling me you don't want no problems. You asked for these problems when you had the notion to step to Ms. Belle. I'm gonna help you out today."

Mrs. Taylor gasped and seemed shocked that I clapped back. She was a schoolteacher bully who said mean things to people using intimidation tactics. Partly due to her age, she thought the younger teachers would take her crap because she was an elder. She was not used to people standing up to her. However, she was just an elder bully. She was popular for the wrong reason. She prided herself on "telling other staff off and putting them in their places." A few months ago, Ms. Taylor yelled at one of our science teachers in front of her students. The poor lady was six months pregnant and went out on maternity leave early because she was so upset with Ms. Taylor's actions. She didn't even complain to the principal or the union. She left one day and did not come back. She faxed in a letter from her doctor that she had to go on bed rest for the rest of the pregnancy. Snow actually replaced her.

Ms. Taylor made one last remark, "I don't know who you are talking to, but I don't have to take this from you. Believe Mr. Lawrence will hear about this."

My feet were moving before my mouth was. "Don't you have an episode of *My 600-lb Life* to record or something? Now get the hell out of my room," I demanded.

Both of the ladies gave me the most sinister look before they turned around in unison and exited my classroom. I was beyond angry. How dare these bitches run up on me like that? I wanted to physically fight them both.

I was too irritated to continue grading papers, so I packed everything up. I had to strategize with Coia. Then the thought hit me. Oh god, if I get Coia involved, it's going to go from 0 to 100 around here. They asked for it; I owe it to them—well, Mrs. Taylor anyway.

It was the end of the day on a Friday. I decided to leave that information for after school. I needed to cool off, and Coia would have talked me into meeting both of Diana Ross and Respusia in the parking lot for an ass whoppin'.

Keith and I weren't speaking, so I could not run to him to let him know what happened. He is buddy-buddy with that stupid-ass Mrs. Taylor; her deceitful ass will tell him all types of lies and conjure up some preposterous tale that I cursed her out and threw a stapler at her. The lapdog that came with her was probably there just for the purpose of collaborating the lies. I hated those mean-ass hags, seriously. It all made sense. They were all working together to fuck with me. Somehow they knew that Keith and I had a fling. His dumb ass would never believe the shit she was doing, nor would he care.

I went to my car and sat inside for a moment. I found my Apple music app and selected "Set It Off" by Lil Boosie to get my mind right. I needed to blow off some of that steam. Boosie did a pretty good job of expressing how I felt.

The ride to the girls' school was extremely tranquil. That hour gave me exactly what I needed to plan. I pulled into the pickup loop. My babies were standing there on the curb beside Ms. Nicholas, lookin' rough but adorable.

Mia ran to the car. She opened the door then ran back to give her teacher a hug. Nia ran to the car. She hopped in the front seat and gave me a bear hug. I needed that.

"Hey, Mommy, I missed you today. We had banana loaf for lunch, and I saved you a piece," Nia said to me. She pulled out a small plastic bag crumpled up in her little shorts pocket. It was almost unrecognizable. Nia put the crumbled cake in my hand. Something so small meant the world to me.

"Thank you, pumpkin, I love it. I am going to eat it all up later," I said gratefully. I once read that when a child gives you a present, no matter how small or insignificant it may seem, it's a treasure that they chose to give to you. I love my baby, but I was not about to eat that li'l germ cake. Nia changed my whole mood. Mia was in the back seat fumbling with my phone. That little slickster went into my purse while I was distracted with Nia and got my phone. She is a bold little girl.

"Mama, you got two text messages," she said without thinking she would get into trouble. This kid is smart, and she is the one I have to watch closely. One day she may commit a blue-collar crime; I need to get ahold of this.

"Mia, get out of my purse and put my phone down. I told you about going through my phone, you li'l crook," I said. "The last time you had my phone, you did something really bad." She quickly put it back, realizing that she could get a spanking this time.

We headed to the grocery store for my mom. We got to her house. The girls jumped out of the car before I did because that was their second home. My mom, Denise Belle, was a character. She was a no-nonsense kind of lady with a great sense of humor and the temper of a rattlesnake. All my friends loved her because she loved music, dancing, and partying. But anyone who knew Denise Belle understood she would chew you up and spit you out if you got her wrong. I needed a dose of raw and uncut today. That meant that I would have to come clean. Mama could tell there was something wrong with me.

She hugged the girls and told them to go inside and get a snack. I walked in behind them with my shoulders slumped and head down as if life had just beat the shit out of me. It actually had.

"Girl, what is wrong with you? This can't be my daughter coming in here with your head down looking lost," she said disappointed.

I sat down in the living room while Mama assisted the girls in the kitchen. The news was on TV, but I could not concentrate on the local news. My mama walked over to me and handed me a glass of orange juice and three shortbread cookies. I loved that snack as a kid.

"Well, Ma, I messed up," I said.

"What do you mean? You broke the law and murdered somebody? Messed up like what?" she asked.

"No, no, it's nothing like that. I had a brief affair with my principal, which turned out to be a disaster. Now his new girlfriend is doing everything she can to infuriate me, including playing with my money," I summarized.

Mama just sat there and looked at me for about two minutes.

"That was stupid as fuck. How did you think that was going to turn out for you? Did he promise you a high position or something? I guess you beat yourself up enough. You can still recover from this," she said.

I was surprised because I expected more of the stupid-as-fuck conversation. Instead she was solution-focused.

"The first thing we have to do is get your money right. Then, we need to get this bitch off your back and make that nigga regret the day he decided to cross you," she said emphatically.

It made sense. She was not going to allow me to be a victim. I told her that I had the money part covered. The topic of the extra jobs came up by default. Since I did not have that extra income any-more, I would have to find another hustle.

I felt so much better to have her in my corner. Denise had her own way of dealing with deceitful people.

"Wait, so what about Kade? Does he know any of this?" Mama asked. She then went on to warn me that he is a rare breed and I was going to lose him if I did not get my shit together. She was right, and I needed to hear that.

I heard a loud scream come from the back of the house. The girls and I looked confused, but Mama seemed to be apathetic. "That's just your daddy, girl. He probably fell out of the bed again. Last week rescue had to come pick his crazy ass off of the floor twice," she replied, unconcerned.

We ran back to his room to see what was wrong. Indeed, he had fallen on the side of his bed. "Help, help, Celeste, help me. I can't get up," my dad said.

He could not get up because he was trapped between the bed and the wall. He lay there stuck on his side, yelling like a crazy person.

Mia went around where she could face him. "Papa, you alright? What you doing down there?" she asked.

Lord, even my baby knew this was ridiculous. Rescue got there in fifteen minutes and helped my dad up off the floor and into a chair. Daddy was looking around lost and disheveled. He did not say much. He just sat there in the chair. Rescue left shortly after. My mama's face said she was sick of that shit.

"Is his dementia and Parkinson's getting worse?" I asked.

"Every fucking day, that shit gets worse," Mama answered, very frustrated.

"The other day, your daddy told me to duck down on the floor 'cause Red Boy and his gang had guns outside of our house. Who the fuck is Red Boy? It wasn't a soul standing outside of our house," she rambled on in frustration.

We made sure that Mama and Daddy were both okay then headed home for the night.

No Smoke

Before school started, we had to cast our votes for Teacher of the Year. I was *so* not in the mood for that shit. I wrote Ms. Edwards's name on the nomination form. Sequoia Edwards was absolutely crazy, but she was brilliant. Her students always had the highest reading gains in the school. With all her insanity, she understood how to provide the tools necessary to help her students show reading growth. As I sat down to complete the full nomination, Ms. Snow, along with Mrs. Taylor, walked in the teacher's lounge laughing as loudly as they could. I'm pretty sure they were stalking me and saw me walk in. They wanted to agitate me. So, they did just that.

Ms. Snow had on a brown-and-white fitted dress with yellow shoes that had no purpose. They looked like grandma shoes. But if that's what Keith wanted, "a grandma-shoe-wearing, no-style-having-ass bitch," he got it! Perhaps if she had a yellow belt and yellow accessories to pull the yellow in, it would have made sense to me. The dress was decent but still lacked style, a basic bitch. That's what bothered me.

Mrs. Taylor had enough sense to not say anything to me directly. She had on an entire blue tent for a dress and flat orthopedic shoes. It's hard to be a bad bitch when you got gout! She and Ms. Snow tried to be indirect.

"Girl, you know you are going to win Teacher of the Year. Mr. Lawrence loves your work," Mrs. Taylor said.

I knew they were trying to get under my skin.

"I hope so. Mr. Lawrence always brings visitors in my class to see my students," she added, trying to throw shade. She wanted me to know that Keith was always in her classroom.

I completed my form. As I got up to place the form in the box, they both watched me and my fitted black slacks that hugged my Coke bottle shape. They were high-waist pants with a large red belt. I had the red button up shirt with a bow that tied to the side of the neck. I had to be careful because I could not fuck up and fall in front of these two awful degenerates. So I took my time in my red platform peep toes that fastened around the ankle. I sat it in the box, monitoring those bitches closely. I was not beneath fighting at work if some shit jumped off. I lifted my red Chanel bag off the table and proceeded in the direction of the door.

One second later, the door to the lounge suddenly swung open; it was Coia. That made me very happy. She came in like a tornado. "What's up, Ms. Belle?" she yelled. It did not take her long to pick up on the tension in the room.

"Everything good, best friend?" she asked while looking directly at Mrs. Taylor and Ms. Snow. Neither one of them wanted to get into a disagreement with Sequoia Edwards. The entire school knew she was a loose cannon with no filter.

I joined in. "Of course, everything is golden. When you look this good, how can it not be?" I said, just to irritate those bitches.

"That outfit is hella cute. I will give you that," she exaggerated.

Mrs. Taylor gave a real stank face when Coia gave me a compliment. Ms. Snow rolled her eyes at both of us. They tried to strike up a fake conversation. But they were still standing there, watching our exchange.

"Oh okay, 'cause I thought it was a two-on-one situation that I needed to get into," she said, just to make it clear.

"Not today, perhaps another time," I responded.

Ms. Snow and Mrs. Taylor saw that things were getting mildly confrontational with Sequoia and decided to retreat. They both left the teacher's lounge pretending to talk about a student in their class.

After they left, Coia was still angry.

"They are lucky that I did not address that situation of Taylor coming in your room. I know Snow tacky, jealous ass was the one behind that shit. And let's not forget the lost checks. They won't get any more passes! The time will come. But, not today." She was beside herself when I told her what the old school twins tried.

"Sometimes you got to show a muthafucka that you are a muthafucka too. And I'm here for it," she said with pride.

Then our conflict started.

"You do know that y'all beefing over a married nigga that have a wife, kids, and other women," she said with irritation.

Coia was right. She was crazy and wild, but right! I hated Keith even more for being the source of drama in my life. I didn't even want to fuck with him anymore. I wanted to teach without either of them bothering me.

I was about to finish up second period. I got a call from the principal's secretary. She sounded like she was almost in a panic. "You have some guests up here waiting on you. They said it's an emergency," she said.

That was strange because I was not expecting anyone, unless it was the district union representative. I trotted down the stairs and headed down the hall. Once I stepped inside, I saw that four very tall guys dressed in street attire. They were in sneakers, hats turned backward, and baggy, sagging jeans. All four of them were six feet tall or bigger. It was scary as fuck.

It was my brother and three cousins. They came unannounced. "Celeste, Mama told me you were having some problems up here. I thought I would stop by to let them know. You the wrong sister to fu—mess with," he said.

Apparently, that comment got Keith's attention. He came out of his office and looked around. "Mrs. Gladys, is everything alright out here?" he asked.

We both turned in Keith's direction and said at the same time, "Everything is fine."

I thought it appropriate to introduce my brother and cousins to Keith. "Mr. Lawrence, this my older brother and my cousins. They were in the area and decided to check on me after the fall and all," I said with a smirk on my face.

My bother, Jerald, did not shake hands at all; he nodded his head up and down, sizing Keith the entire time.

"I was just about to walk them out," I said. Jerald and my cousins strolled out of the office looking like they were straight outta Compton, not cracking a smile or speaking. As we walked out to the parking lot, people in the hall paused and stared as we left the building. I could hear the PE coach saying, "Damn, who they came here to kill?"

As soon as we reached the steps outside, Jerald said, "Ma told me that bitch-ass nigga was giving you a hard time. I ain't come up here to start a fight and go to jail today. But, I wanted his ass to know you got a crazy-ass brother that will fuck him up if anything else happens."

"Oh lord, Mama sent y'all." I should have known. I burst out laughing. That was right up her alley. I appreciated the gesture even if it was crazy. I hugged all four of them.

I held my hand out. "Now which one of y'all paying for my lunch, fa real?" I asked. Jerald took a fifty-dollar bill out of his pocket and told me to get me and the twins something to eat later.

They headed back to the parking lot, and I returned to go back in the building. Keith was still standing in the hall, trying to figure out why my brother and cousins showed up at my place of employment. Denise Belle was not beneath intimidation tactics.

I walked right past him in the hall along with a few other teachers looking stupid in the face.

That little trick made my day. I found it amusing.

On my way home, Kade called.

"Celeste, we need to talk. Is tonight good with you?" he asked.

The girls were settled in their room. I was in a decent mood despite everything happening at work. Kade came in looking good in crisp white jeans and a navy-blue-and-white polo shirt. He was such a cutie. He threw his keys on the table and sat next to me.

"You have been too busy to talk and spend time with me. I love you, but I'm not a man that's going to beg. I have options just like you have options," he said.

I could not tell him that I had been distracted because I had a messy affair with my principal and we broke up. So I had to be smart about this. He was a lawyer whose job was to seek the truth.

"Babe, you are right. I have not been giving you the attention that you deserve. I'm sorry. I underestimated the work and energy involved in working at a title 1 school," I responded.

"Wow, you have been working at the same school since I met you, so that argument won't hold. I'm a lawyer, stop. I saw the look your principal gave you when I dropped you off to work that morning. When I put your card and money in your suitcase, I saw all the sexy lingerie and panties you packed. Who were you packing those for? Not me. Whatever is going on with you is personal, and I'm going to give you the space you need to figure that shit out," he said.

Kade stood up, took my house keys off his key ring, and left them on my counter. He walked to the door without looking back and left. I felt so numb. I felt hurt, but it was not the hurt I felt at school. I was accustomed to disappointment by now. I didn't expect him or any other man to stay around.

At 3:00 a.m., my phone had a text alert. It was something stupid from a marketing company. I woke up and realized that Kade was gone. I could not call him anymore when I needed a ride, to pick up the girls, or to hang out with. I took him for granted, and he wasn't having that shit. Once it all came to me, I cried in my pillow. It was really Kade's pillow. That was his side of the bed. He was always there for me. He did not deserve to be treated like this.

THE TRIFLING PRINCIPAL

The reality that Kade left me lingered over me. The idea of it made me feel sad and empty.

I went to Nikki's class for lunch. We all ate lunch in her class together.

"Kade came over last night to break things off," I said.

"I told your simple ass that Kade was a good man and not to fuck it up," Nikki said.

"I was caught up in the thrill of fucking with Keith. The shit didn't work out, and I lost Kade. Dumbest shit ever! To top it off, I'm at war with some stupid bitch I don't even know," I added.

There was no sympathy in the room. They knew Kade deserved better, and I knew it too.

The school days were flying by. I seemed so detached from teaching.

It was third period, and I had two more periods to go. The bell could not ring soon enough to dismiss the students. I said all my goodbyes and homework requests. As soon as the hall was clear, I did a fast jog down two flights of stairs, papers flying behind me as I swung my satchel behind my back to gain more speed. My cell phone, wallet, and brush were hanging on for dear life at the mouth of my purse. With a brief pause, I attempted to zip my purse. I thought I was home-free and headed to the car. I knew I smelled the rank stench of a cow; my archenemy was standing before me. Why was this bitch even this close to me, just to be an asshole? I tried to ignore her. Satan was so busy.

Not caring that I was in a hurry at all, she tried to physically block the stairway with her body. I was in an impossible position. I could not get down the staircase.

I looked down at her and said, "Excuse you, could you NOT block the stairwell?" Number A, she was dressed in a dark-green skirt and a dark-green shirt with absolutely no hairstyle at all. She looked like a skinny forest tree. To add, she had on the world's worst run-over shoes. *Bitch, you can't have a friend in this world to let you dress like that*, I thought.

Ms. Snow demanded, "I need to talk to you, now!"

"I am going to say this one more time: move out of the way, or I'm going to knock you out of the way, it's just that simple," I said, very disturbed.

"You think you are slick, but Keith don't want you. So, you can stop throwing yourself at him. I know that you still call him all the time," she said with attitude.

"You tacky-dressed toad, I don't give a damn about you or Keith or anyone else. Kermit, hop your ass out of my way," I insisted.

She refused to move. No one else was in the hall at the moment. Ms. Snow postured herself closer to me. She was directly in front of me. Ms. Snow gathered a grin on her face that invited the wrath of evil. She did not say a word, but she did not move either.

Just then, it all came to a head—the drama, the hospital, my checks, and Kade. Now this bitch wouldn't move. Before I could even think, I pushed forward, running into her chest. With my hands extended and the power of gravity behind me, Ms. Snow flew backward. She tumbled down a half flight of stairs landing on her "flat ass." She hit the floor so hard that she slid into the glass trophy case like a bowling ball.

The timing could not have been worse; her heroic boyfriend, a.k.a. Principal Lawrence, a.k.a. Keith's bitch ass, was close in proximity when she fell. Ms. Snow then let out a loud scream, "She pushed me, she pushed me!" She began to fake cry. He ran to her rescue.

"Ms. Belle cursed at me and pushed me down the steps! I want her arrested!"

Crying uncontrollably, Mr. Lawrence helped her up off the ground and dusted her skirt off. Ms. Snow staggered to steady herself and continued crying while maintaining a firm grip on Mr. Lawrence's arm.

The principal looked up at me in disgust. He straightened his coat jacket, squinted his eyes, and in a very firm voice, asked, "Did you push Ms. Snow?"

I did not know how to answer that. I mean I did push her, but she would not move. We both know that I did not push her down the stairs. I just pushed her out of my way.

Still processing what happened, I belted, "No, not really. Not the way she said it," I added. Just that quick, I thought, *Maybe I should have denied the whole thing.* Mr. Lawrence was a light-complexioned man. His face was the color of a red apple.

"In my office now, Ms. Belle!" Mr. Lawrence bellowed. So much for my plan to get home early!

Instead of walking to his office with me, he had to stay behind and babysit this silly bitch who started it all. The only thing she hurt was her damn ego. She should not have postured herself in front of me. She knew exactly what she was doing! I walked into Mr. Lawrence's office like a first grader getting in trouble for fighting. My purse and satchel were still on my shoulder barely moving. I walked slowly to the set of chairs that faced his desk. I filled the time by looking at pictures of his wife and children, wondering if they had a happy life like the pictured portrayed.

My attention immediately went to the floor, where he dropped his business cards, and we were intimate for the first time. I thought of the closet adjacent to his desk where we would have our secret meetings, him with no tie, me with a dress and no panties. My mind thought back to the day after my civics scores were public. They were the second highest in the district. Keith told me that he had a surprise for me. I was superexcited. I washed up in the teachers' bathroom using my sample-size bodywash and Victoria's Secret lotion. I went in his office after a late parent meeting that evening, leaving a trail of "smell good" behind my every step. One foot in his office, he came up behind me, swept me up by my waist, and led me to the closet, leaning me over the table.

Keith and I were so close; how did we get here? He was seeing about another woman while I was sitting in his office, awaiting punishment; it seemed so backward.

After almost three and a half years, this asshole decided to act I'm not shit. "Are you serious?" Well, that was a big damn mistake. I looked over at my phone to find a message from my mom.

Hi, CC, just calling to check when you were going to drop the girls off. I miss them. Mia's supposed to help me plant my garden. Call me when you get this message, and Big Mama has already told you to call her twice.

I needed to call them both back, but this shit was *so* damn distracting. I hated this bastard right now. Keith came into his office and closed his door pretty hard. I guess that was supposed to intimidate me.

"There are no words that can describe how angry I am that you would do something like this," he said like I was a child.

I was so mad. I could not help but yell, "She initiated all of this shit! She thinks I have something going with you."

Keith took his time explaining that there was certainly nothing between us or her. He then dropped the hammer.

"After reviewing the security camera in the hallway, it seems that you pushed her. Although she was standing in your way, you could have turned around and walked in the opposite direction. You pushed her on purpose. Ms. Snow could have been seriously hurt. You have two choices. You can apologize, or I am going to have to suspend you with no pay for the next three days," he stated with pleasure.

"What, suspend me? Like a student, suspension?" I asked, puzzled.

"I tell you what, Mr. Lawrence, I will walk from here to South Beach Miami, buy a broom along the way, and sweep the entire beach before I apologize to that witch."

"Three days it is! This will give you some time to reflect on your actions," he added.

I did not even waste time arguing with his stupid ass. How fucking dare he do this to me. Maybe I did push that bitch, but she deserved it. *Oh god, this couldn't be real,* I thought.

I was gonna have to call Kade; now I was one of those teachers who has to fight administration because of this bullshit. How was I gonna make this all logical without admitting to the affair? I texted Coia from the parking lot.

Since it was after school, she scurried down to the parking lot fairly quickly. I had to literally stop her from going back in the building to confront Kermit, the damn frog, and Mr. Lawrence's bitch ass.

"Celeste, what happened?" Coia asked seriously. I tried to explain what happened when Ms. Snow confronted me and stood in my way. I did admit to pushing her, but not down the stairs. Coia was proud. She high-fived me in the parking lot. I was crying with my right hand up to receive her high five. Coia hugged me.

"It's okay, boo, that bitch got what she deserved. Don't feel bad for that shit. Fuck him and her! That nigga better be glad we not going to the union on his ass for sexual harassment for all of those times he got too comfortable with you," she implied. She was trying to set the scene for me being the victim.

I felt so hurt and betrayed. I calmed down just a tad bit as Coia boxed around the parking lot pretending to be a professional boxer. She started throwing punches, jumping around like she was knocking the shit out of Keith and Snow. I laughed and cried at the same time. I really needed to talk to legal, Kade. I wasn't sure if Keith or Snow was going to take this much further. I had to prepare myself in case I needed to hire a separated lawyer.

REUNITED

I had the next three days off. I desperately needed legal counsel. Kade would be useful, but we weren't on good terms. What was I going to tell them? I pushed another teacher down the stairs because she was sleeping with my married ex-boyfriend? The whole ordeal was an unadulterated mess. I lay back in my bed, staring at the ceiling. The girls had a birthday coming up in a few weeks. Since I had the time, I thought perhaps it was a small blessing. I rarely get time without the girls to go shopping.

I went to Walmart and threw Barbies, clothes, furniture, and all other types of baby items in my basket. I remember Kade said he got them bicycles. It would be awkward asking him for the bikes, so I contemplated getting them bikes.

The phone rang. I recognized the tone of that voice anywhere. I had not heard from him since Vegas. It was Dereck.

"Hi there, beautiful. I told you in the email I would be in Florida in a couple of months. Here I am," he said. He was in town on business.

I wanted to forget about the real world for a few days, maybe even a few hours.

I answered, "Hey, stranger, how are you? Great to hear from you."

Before I could finish with my pleasantries, Dereck responded, "I missed you, Celeste, come see Daddy."

That tingle traveled from my breasts to the center of my womanhood. Quickly, I had to figure out what to wear that would give him easy access but still would still look supersexy. Turquoise, yes! I had to find my long maxi dress with the split. It was in the closet next to my yellow blazer. I was fantasizing thinking how great this afternoon was going to be with Dereck. I found the matching hot-pink bra-and-panty set that accentuated my physique and complimented the turquoise.

A few hours later, I met Dereck at his hotel on the beach. I knocked on the door. My heart beat like I was a teenager in high school. He was so sexy. Dereck had on tailored navy blue pants, a white button-up shirt and matching blue suspenders. He had the body of a football god. Every muscle bulged from his tailored suit, including his man stick. It was those thick dark eyebrows that got me the first time. I was reminded why I ditched Keith in Vegas to sneak around with Dereck. At this moment, I did not regret it. I looked into his eyes with those long lashes, and he grabbed me by my waist. We kissed for at least five minutes.

"You are breathtaking baby, just striking," he said. I turned around to give him a full view of all this milk chocolate. His tie was loosened. He took the tie from around his neck and put it around mine.

"I'm not sure if this matches my outfit, love," I responded.

"Take off the dress and panties. The tie is your outfit," he said with a smile.

Dereck unbuttoned his shirt completely with his chest exposed. He removed his pants but kept his boxers on. Dereck reached under my dress and pulled my panties off with one tug. He put them in his shirt pocket. Dereck sat down on the couch with his large penis exposed. I walked over to join him. He gently sat me on his lap so that I could position myself for insertion. His erect shaft fit perfectly inside me. Although I was on top, Dereck still did the driving. He held my hips firmly and held them down for pressure. He then fucked me from the bottom. I turned around in reverse cowgirl style. He enjoyed that immensely. His toes began to curl. He held me tightly and let out a loud roar. I was not done.

The day was still young. I got into the shower and wore one of Dereck's shirts around the room. He sat in the bed flipping through channels. I plopped down on the bed beside him. He had lunch ordered for us both. He was such a gentleman.

"So how is Keith? I haven't spoken to him in a while," Dereck asked. He was trying to see if we were still fucking around.

"We are not on good terms right now. After Vegas, he figured out that someone else had my attention. It caused major problems with us," I explained.

"Well, who had your attention, Ms. Belle?" he asked.

I put my head on his shoulder and said, "You, Dereck."

He laid me down and licked me slowly. He used his fingers and tongue like a synchronized machine. I climaxed in five minutes flat.

We ate lobster salad and crab cakes for lunch while enjoying each other's company. I left him feeling like a new woman. He was just what the doctor ordered.

I left the hotel and went to my aunt Carol's house. She picked the girls up early from school and took them to Children's Museum. Both Nia and Mia had face paint all over their cheeks. They had bags full of cotton candy, popcorn, and chocolate. It was the most perfect day for two six-year-olds. I wanted to get them home before it got too late. It was time to go. Mia gave Carol a bear hug around the neck, almost knocking her over as she bent down to hug her aunt back. Nia was content with grabbing Carol's leg and not letting go. Carol walked back to the car with Nia on her leg and Mia's hand wrapped around her finger.

Screaming at the same time, "Can we go to the zoo next time, please, please?" Nia and Mia asked in an alternating pattern. "Are we going to see the animals? Can I touch a giraffe? Do they have ice cream at the zoo?"

Mia interjected with a moment of seriousness, "Do you think a lion will eat us, Aunt Carol?"

Aunt Carol, just as excited as the girls, replied, "Girls, I heard that they have biggest, smartest animals ever in this zoo. The animals are so smart that they talk."

The girls, in disbelief, said, "No way... Animals cannot talk." They got into the car. Ten minutes later, they were asleep. Before Aunt Carol left, I put all of the twins' birthday presents in her car so they would not see them.

I took a chance and called Kade anyway. I needed the help of a lawyer.

"Hello," Kade answered.

I paused for a minute. "It's me, Kade. I got into some trouble at work, and I just need your professional opinion, if you have a moment," I requested.

"Alright, come by the office tomorrow and we can discuss the case," he stated. His office? I thought for sure he would come over to the house. I was kind of hoping he would at least offer to meet me somewhere to discuss it. Damn, I had lost Kade completely.

Day two of my suspension and I went to the legal office. I was not about to be the punching bag for Keith's ego or Snow's insecurity.

The office had no parking. I had to walk a quarter mile just to get a space. The office was fairly quiet and empty with the exception of the lawyers working on various cases. I entered the building and asked to speak with Mr. Capshaw.

Kade came out looking super dapper with his work attire. I forgot what a great dresser he was. He took a folder off the receptionist's desk and called me back. "Ms. Belle, come with me, please."

I had been contemplating how much I was going to divulge.

I got to his office. It was plain with no decorations or wall décor. He had his law degree and undergrad degree framed on a bookshelf behind his desk. I thought he would at least have a picture of me or the twins. Nothing!

"Okay, Celeste, what is going on that you need legal consultation?" he questioned.

"Well, Kade, for the past three months, I have been working in a hostile work environment. The principal's groupies have confronted me in my classroom, in the hallway, purposely lost my check, and even left me on the floor to die," I protested.

"What reason would the principal or his groupies have for harassing you, causing a hostile work environment?" he probed.

Again he was not a stupid man. I just could not tell him everything. He had actually figured it all out before he left me. I prepared to give him more details when a young attractive lady walked into his office without knocking on the door. She barged in as if she was in a hurry.

She was Spanish. Her hair was a midnight black with thick curls that hung to her breasts. She was dressed appropriately for a lawyer with a nice shape. Even her shoes coordinated with her dress. I was impressed.

"Mr. Capshaw, do you have any settlement agreements?" she asked seductively.

Kade pointed over his shoulder and motioned for her to go inside the file cabinet to get it herself. She had to be very comfortable with Kade to march in his office and squeeze her ass behind his chair to get documents. I know he was attracted to her because she was a very pretty lady.

I presume he did have other options. I felt like a stranger in his office. I made the choice to leave and deal with my own problems at work.

She squeezed back behind his chair, making sure they had physical contact before exiting his office. Kade did not bother to introduce us. I took that as a sign to leave.

"Maybe I'm just overreacting," I admitted. I picked my purse up and left abruptly.

"I can drop the girls' bicycles off to your mother's house if that's okay with you," he added. I nodded as I departed.

DOWNHILL

It had been two weeks since I said a word to Keith. He walked past me in the hallway like I was furniture in the middle of the room. I did the same. Ms. Snow seemed to have a new sense of confidence, perhaps arrogance about her. She figured that she had Keith wrapped around her dirty, unmanicured fingers. She literally thought of herself as the queen of the school. Everyone noticed, and it pissed me off. I am not sure if I was more upset that she took my spot or the fact that she was trying to rub it in my face. I had been thrown aside like an old dust rag. I mean, Ms. Snow is a pretty lady, but she was unintelligent, plain, and unprofessional. She could not put an outfit together if her life depended on it. She needed to settle her ass down.

It was a teacher planning day. We had a meeting that morning in the media center. The only reason I showed up instead of taking leave was because I needed to know more information about the upcoming school budget and how it would impact me personally. I sat down beside two teachers who had a hard time "keeping it together," Nikki and Coia. I needed that distraction. The crazier they acted, the more the attention stayed off me and my sorted love triangle.

Of course, this fake bitch, Ms. Snow, walked in as if she were royalty. To her credit, she had on a nicely shaded pink body-con dress with taupe shoes to match for a change. I guess her dumb ass can coordinate colors. Her hair seemed more groomed than usual instead of that tired flat wrap she had been wearing. As she passed through the checkout counter of the library, she wanted to make sure that I saw her. She pressed herself against two tables. Her ridiculous ass boldly blurted, "Make room for the queen." I could have thrown up right then and there! Queen where? Granted, she was an attractive woman; she always seemed dirty to me. In the words of my crazy big mama, the seat of her panties probably nastier than summer trash sitting outside. I was thoroughly confused; how did Keith leave expensive perfumes, impeccable wardrobe, and beauty for a dirty bitch? That made me even more upset, but I had to get through this meeting. I didn't even want Keith anymore. My pride was hurt.

Coia and Nikki could not wait for the meeting to start before they launched into "It's not fair to even consider cutting math or English positions." They supported their argument with the shortage of teachers, underfunding for the school as it is, and the fact that our reading and math scores were not as high as most. All were good points, but when it comes to funding public schools, the federal and state government could give less than a damn if kids are hurt academically. It's is a sad state of affairs when politics overrides the well-being of children, especially black and brown kids. I hate Republicans!

Mr. Lawrence walked in still fine but less attractive for having poor taste in women. He had on a black suit that fit his athletic body from the top to the bottom. Then he fucked it up with some scuffed-up shoes that looked like they belonged to his great-granddaddy. Seriously, buy some damn shoes. If you want to act like top dog, then dress the part.

I was so glad no one spoke to me directly. It had to be all over my face: "Today you will get the full business if you mess with me." No-filter Friday, who wants it?

Mr. Lawrence pulled out a notebook with loose papers dangling outside it. He pulled one sheet out as he welcomed us to all sit and begin the meeting.

"As you all know, it is that time of year where we have to make some decisions about next year's budget," Mr. Lawrence explained as he continued with his rehearsed speech.

"We will be losing some teachers next year due to the recent budget cuts that came directly from the State of Florida. Our governor does not believe in funding much for public schools, which means much our money has been reallocated to private and charter schools." That's one thing we agree on; the government hates public education!

"Unfortunately, I have to make cuts in almost every department." He began to spout out English, math, science, social studies, and electives. Of course, that's all the teachers needed to hear to start up a mini riot! We all began talking over one another in anguish and disgust because it was mutual that this was jacked up. Each table had its own conversation of disdain going, all while Mr. Lawrence attempted to calm the crowd. So of course, the old school twins sitting across from me asked the question of the day: who is going to be fired? When you have thirty years plus with the school board, you can ask shit like that. One of the ladies declared in resentment: we have families, we have kids, we need to know which one of us has to go. Mr. Lawrence took a momentary pause. He looked down at his pad that was inside his notes. "The administrators and myself have come up with a list of names of those who won't be returning next year. We will ask those who want to voluntarily leave to please submit those transfers to us now, and perhaps that would save a few teaching positions." Mr. Lawrence seemed slightly annoyed by the lack of response. No one raised their hands, and no one seemed interested at leaving at that moment. "There will be a total of seven positions lost. I need the following teachers to please stay behind after the meeting." It did not take a genius to know what that was about. The teachers staying behind were the ones who were getting the "axe." My heart was beating so fast because I know we had bad blood. I was not sure if Ms. Dirty Panties herself tried to convince Mr. Lawrence to surplus me. The uncertainty was killing me.

He started reading off names, "Mr. Reed, I need you to stay. Mrs. Wright, I need you to stay." Jones paused.

My heart was still beating fast. "Okay, that's two, and he said seven positions," I convinced myself.

"Mrs. Wilder, Ms. Reed, and Mr. Jennings, I need you three to stay behind as well," Mr. Jones detailed. You could hear a pin drop in the room because he was not holding back with cutting positions. We all knew there were two names to go.

Mr. Lawrence appeared stressed and said in a very low tone, "Ms. Parker and Ms. Belle, I also need you ladies to stay behind." I felt it in my heart. I knew he would pull this bullshit. The entire room seemed to look at the teachers who had been called as if we had some contagious disease and needed to be contained in a secluded room. I could have killed that bastard then and there. All that we had been through and done to make shit happen for this same school. This shit is personal! If he wants to make it personal, let's do that! I had to keep my composure because this had to be carefully calculated. He expected me to "pop off" and curse him out in front of all these people so I could lose my certification. Not today, bitch! Stay tuned.

I went through my mental breakdown internally; all the others were exiting the room, hugging the exiting teachers. This prompted Mr. Lawrence to make another statement, "Teachers, please understand this was beyond my control. You are being surplused, not fired. You will be moved to another school within the district for the next school year."

He could have kept that dumb shit to himself. Six of the teachers that were asked to stay did exactly as told and followed Mr. Lawrence to his office. I made sure he saw that I could not give a flying fuck about going to his office. I was going to get my girls early and deal with this bullshit when I could think straight. Fuck him. He could get somebody else to cover my class tomorrow, as a matter of fact. I needed a minor sabbatical. I'm not even calling in a substitute teacher. The sorry bastard needs to make it work. Coia and Nikki went up to him, pleading my case without my permission. I had no desire to teach another year under him. I left the school altogether without saying anything to anyone. However, it was no secret I was livid and was leaving for the rest of the day to cool off.

It occurred to me that my aunt had the twins today. I had some time to kill. I had the day from hell. I did not want to see anyone from work. We went to a pub way on the other side of town with Coia and Nikki.

We went inside and ordered food and alcoholic beverages at the bar. It was hard to fellowship and laugh with so much going on at work. I had the pleasure of knowing I did not have to see Keith or Snow the following school year. Finally, I accepted the consequence.

Coia turned around. "Celeste, is that Kade with that lady sitting over there?" she said.

I turned my head in the same direction. Kade sat there in a corner booth with the same lawyer from his office. I put that together when I was in his office. I could not be mad at him. Nikki slid a drink in my direction. "I told you not to fuck it up," she said.

What else, Lord? My life is falling apart by the day.

DISCLOSURE

Today was our girlfriends' meeting at Nikki's house. It was tradition to get together with the girls and talk about all the shit with the school board. We usually worked our way from individual schools to the head district office.

"Girl, I heard that the deputy superintendent has a girlfriend, a wife, and a lover. Last month, the lady in benefits told me that the wife came in and shut all that shit down," Coia said.

"Wait though, isn't the wife good friends with the lover or she was at some point?" I interjected. How can I talk about anyone? My married ex-boyfriend just fired me and sent me packing.

Seriously, Coia continued, "The wife showed up at the main school board and jumped on him in the elevator. She had to be escorted out by police. It embarrassed the shit out of him."

"You know how that shit goes. They all sleep their way to the top till the shit get bad, doleful snakes," Nikki said in a curt tone. "Can't trust none of them."

"But the meeting last week was a catastrophe. How are you dealing with that, Celeste?" Nikki asked. I felt as though I was the new charity case of the school.

"I'm fine. I am not the first teacher to be surplused, and I'm not the last," I said with little sarcasm.

They continued with the "Did you know…" conversations. I tuned out for a few minutes in disbelief that all this was happening to me.

Business had to go on. The next day, I went down to the school board to look for the hiring list for next year. It was important that I tone the sexy down; I did not want to give the impression that I was a "sexpot" as my big mama would say.

As I entered the elevator, I saw the sharp-dressed lady from the store. I think she recognized me as well. I wondered what she was doing in the school board office. She was surrounded by several other people. Her heels were low and comfortable. Her hair was swept up in a messy bun. She had a friendly face. I witnessed her walk into an office with the name Meredith Reyes. I remembered she gave me her business card when I gave her the wallet she left behind. I reached into my purse for the card. It took a little digging, but I located it. The card also said "Meredith Reyes, school board member." She was a high-ranking school board member. Mrs. Reyes popped back out of her office and saw me sitting out in the reception area.

"Hi, I would recognize that face anywhere. You saved my life that day in the store!" she exclaimed.

I was truthful. "I am a teacher in Pine River Middle. I am being surplused and have to look for a job opening," I told her. Mrs. Reyes called me to her office. I looked around, and she had pictures with the mayor, other school board members, and various other dignitaries. Mrs. Reyes handed me a list of vacancies to review. Then the questions started.

With everything that was going on, still being suspended, I don't know how or why, but I just started bawling. The flood of tears felt therapeutic. Ms. Reyes gave me tissue. She sat beside me and allowed me to gather myself.

"I'm sorry, I don't ever do this. I really am a great teacher. Right now I am teaching under some really harsh conditions and…" I cried before I had another torrential pour of tears.

"Let's start here," she said. A five-minute meeting of looking for a job turned into a psychiatric session. Mrs. Reyes was completely understanding. She asked me who my principal was and how my experience was. I described the situation in detail. Transparency was important if I wanted her help.

"Ms. Belle, you are young and have a bright future in teacher if you stay focused on teaching. Sadly enough, this is not the first complaint that I have heard about this particular principal," she said surprisingly.

I felt like a huge boulder had been lifted off my back. That boulder had been weighing down on me for a couple of months and became unbearable.

She advised me to go home, rest, and reflect. I genuinely appreciated her advice. My life could truly get back on track. I got up and hugged her. It did not occur to me that it was inappropriate to do so, but she had helped me so much just by listening. She assured me that things would be alright.

As I walked out of the office, Mrs. Reyes indicated that she would call me soon about a position.

It was about 6:00 p.m. My day had been exhausting. Part of me could not believe I cried and confessed to a total stranger. Mostly, I was glad that I did. It felt like an essential purge. All the darkness slowly started to seep out. When I pulled into my driveway, I saw Mama's car. Denise could always sense when something was wrong with her kids. She knew something was going on more serious than she imagined. Mia saw me in through the window and opened the door for me. "Mommy, you're home," she said cheerfully. Mia jumped up and gave me a kiss on my cheek. She held my hand and led me into the living room where Mama was sitting.

"So that sorry-ass principal fired you? Okay. I guess he did not get my first message with your brother," she said like a mobster. She sat there deep in thought. Suddenly she looked at her watch. "Girl, I gotta get home to your daddy before he blows the whole damn place up," she said in a hurry.

"Mama, don't be concerned about this job thing. I'm going to handle it. I talked to someone today," I assured her.

She kissed both of the girls goodbye and hugged me. I walked her to the car and told her to drive carefully.

I had not spent any quality time with my babies, but things had to be in order. I needed Promise to come through for me.

I hesitated to pick up the phone and dialed. He answered in a good mood.

"Promise, it's me. I…I have a lot going on at work. I need you to get the girls for a few days," I pleaded.

"Okay, I need to move a few things around, but it shouldn't be a problem. I will pick them up in the morning," he said willingly.

I was quiet for a moment. "Thank you, Promise, this is really helping me out," I said in a wavering voice. He had also been with me long enough to know something was wrong.

"C, this don't sound like you, what's wrong?" he asked. I couldn't tell him just yet.

But I gave him an honest answer. "Everything is wrong, Promise, I just don't know."

I hung up the phone because I had nothing left to say. Twenty minutes went by.

The girls were quiet and playing in their room. I was sitting up front in the living room. I heard a knock at the door. It was Promise. I could not believe it. What was he doing here unannounced?

"Promise, what are you doing here?" I asked as I opened the door.

He looked at me and could tell I had been crying. Promise hugged me. It felt good and familiar. He was one of my oldest friends and my first love. I was pleased to see him.

The girls heard their daddy's voice and went crazy. Nia ran out of her room with her Barbie in hand.

"Daddy, you came to pick us up?" she asked excitedly.

Mia came running right behind her. "Hey, Daddy, what you doing here at night?" she questioned. They were accustomed to our routine of weekend pickup and drop-off during daytime hours.

"I came to see the most beautiful twins in the world. Your mommy was tired, so I came over to help out," he said.

"Yep, we have to babysit Mommy a lot," Mia said. Kids talk too much! Promise and I laughed hard at that comment. It was an adorable family moment. I was tremendously grateful to have the help.

Promise bathed the girls and got their clothes ready for the next day. I was on the couch in the living room watching a horror movie. That was my go-to. The fear took the focus off my problems. Promise came in to join me. He looked like he had a long day too. We need to talk about the plans for the twins' birthday party. He stopped midsentence. "Are you listening to me?" he asked. I was relieved that I had purchased their presents way before any of this drama started. Promise was in charge of the party location. I ordered the cake, or did I? I couldn't remember.

"You know you scary, why are you watching this shit? Then you'll have all of the lights on in the house," he teased. Promise was actually correct. I love watching scary movies, but they frightened the shit out of me. The strange thing about scary movies was, they allowed me to focus on someone else's dreadful story and not my own. He snuggled next to me and put his head on my shoulder. An hour into the movie, he was snoring. I maneuvered from under him and went to get him a comforter. Promise always complained that I kept the house freezing.

Getting the comforter gave me a chance to go take a hot shower. I reflected for a few minutes. Things were not that bad. I had family and friends. My babies were healthy; everything else would work itself out.

I hopped out of the shower, and everything was dark. Promise woke up and turned all the damn lights off. He knew I just watched a horror movie. I tiptoed through the hallway in the dark like a slasher was in my home. That's why I don't need to watch horror movies. I got to my room and found Promise sprawled across my bed.

"Promise, move over, you are taking up the whole bed, man," I grumbled. He woke up putting his hands all over me.

"Boy, if you don't take your ass to sleep and stop playing," I said. He was still charming, but he was not getting no ass tonight. I put cover on the both of us and went to sleep.

PLANNING PERIOD

The aroma of bacon and eggs worked me out of my sleep. Mia and Nia were dressed in their uniforms and ready for school.

"Good morning, guys. This is a nice surprise," I said to my little family. Mia contested going to school; she wanted to go with her dad. I tried to ignore her request.

"Eat your breakfast, Mia. It will make you big and strong like Daddy," I diverted.

Promise added, "I will get you for the next few days, baby, you and your sister. "We will play UNO, Connect 4, and Barbies." Mia decided that was a good bargain for her. She agreed.

Promise loaded the girls in his truck. Their overnight bags were packed and ready. I kissed all three of them goodbye like I was the doting wife and mother.

I had a *Cosby Show* Bill-and-Claire moment. For twenty-four hours, we were a happy Black family.

I had to face reality. Going back to work was something that I dreaded. I did not want to see Snow or Keith. With any luck, the day would fly by, and I could focus on Mia and Nia's birthday.

Promise had taken the day off to prepare for the girls' big day. He and my mama had to communicate today. That could be a travesty.

I looked down at my phone and saw that Dereck had returned for a back-to-back business tip.

It was my planning. Dereck texted me and said he had great news. He wanted me to meet him.

I couldn't believe I'm doing this on my planning period. I have to learn to calm my hormones down. I have an insatiable craving for peanut butter right now. His skin is smooth, creamy brown. The thought of that thick groomed beard between my thighs made me anxious.

With my care kit in my teachers' tote, I picked it up and scurried through the teachers' lounge before the first wave of teachers began their restroom breaks. I quickly warmed my washcloth with a sample-size bodywash. I took the lathered cloth into the first stall in the girls' room, pulled my lace panties completely off, and slipped them in my bag. They would just get in the way. I think I like this guy more than I thought. Or maybe I liked the thrill of the unplanned sex. *Life was pretty good*, I thought. I was over Keith! I just wanted him and his minion to leave me the fuck alone.

I wondered what Dereck's good news was. I signed out in the secretary's office. The anticipation of seeing Dereck and all ten inches of his dick had me on a natural high.

I had to have him! Even if it was not in my master plan, peanut butter was my new flavor.

Getting in my car, I had to be quick.

I was not prepared for questions from Nikki or Sequoia. Sneaking away on planning was very similar to a situation that I experienced about a year ago.

He was a handsome guy who caught my eye in a student-versus-faculty basketball game. Courtney ran up and down the court in gray sweats. His manhood curved down his leg like a snake in his pants. I followed every move that he made. He noticed that I was watching him. Courtney enjoyed the attention and started showing off. After a victory, he invited me over. I happily accepted. The challenge was, Courtney did not live in the best part of town. In fact, many of my students lived in that area. Our first hookup was stressful. I was scuttled through a playground and housing projects, hoping not to look suspicious enough for the cops to confront me—I was a Black woman in the middle of a housing project; you know the story with police. What if one of my students' parents saw me and asked what I was doing in this area? Shit, what would be my response?

After a slight heart attack, I made it to apartment 309 C. None of that other stuff mattered, at ALL. Peanut butter and chocolate never looked so good together. He was wrapped in a crisp white towel fresh out of the shower. The top of his shoulders were wide and muscular as the midsection formed a V. My eyes took it all in before the bulge underneath that white towel stole the show. Courtney seemed like a soft, feminine name, but he was anything but soft and feminine! By the time my eyes traveled back upward toward his lips, he grabbed me. Game over…he scooped me up and led me to the living room. It was not the time to play shy, so I joined the party. I threw my top on the floor and unfastened my bra.

"*No*, I got that, let me." He ripped the bra off with his teeth. Damn, I needed my bra. How do I go back with the "girls" hanging? Oh well, I couldn't worry about that. Courtney got to my skirt. To his surprise, I had nothing underneath. Panties off, vagina was clean; eat up, handsome. He took a pause to look me in the face with a devious grin. "I like that, Ms. Belle."

I embraced the moment. I locked down and grabbed the top of his head when he put the tip of his tongue on my pearl. It felt *so* good. I had moaned his name before I actually meant for it to be said out loud. By the eighth suck-and-lick combination, I had a tear running down my right eye. It stopped nothing! My legs made an inverted V on his shoulders; my entire middle was in his face, in his mouth. He licked my pearl in rhythm for about eight minutes, then I felt a cold sensation that traveled from my toes to my brain.

Courtney's porno vision put me in the mood to see Dereck. That memory was the perfect segue into my meeting with Dereck. I wanted no interruptions. I left my phone in the car to charge. I was only planning I would not be long. Dereck came to the door and hugged me. "Guess what, I am the new deputy superintendent for Dade County," he said enthusiastically. I saw things looking up for me already. I embraced him. We kissed and made love for at least an hour. I was going to be late going back to work.

This was turning out to be a wonderful day.

CHAPTER BIRTHDAY GIRL

I picked up my phone and saw I had a million messages from Sequoia, Mama, and Promise. They were probably all in a panic about the birthday party. I was not participating in that today.

"Hello, yes, is this the Bakery Department?" I inquired.

"I need to make sure that my cake is ready for pickup. Yes, the name is Celeste Bell," I continued on the call.

"The cake should say, 'Happy Birthday, Nia and Mia,' with a huge Black Barbie in the center and yellow and pink balloons bordering the cake."

Beep. (Someone was trying to reach me on the other line.) It was my mom. I didn't have time to answer. I needed to make sure things were in place for when I picked the girls up.

Beep. The phone rang again. It was Promise again. "What the hell is going on?" I wondered. This was nuts… Before I could sit the phone back down on the seat, Sequoia texted me.

It's an emergency. Call me this second.

"Siri, call Coia."

"Calling Coia."

"Celeste, where are you? Haven't you been watching the news or at least listening to the radio?" she asked frantically on the verge of tears.

"What's wrong? You are acting really strange, Coia. My mama and Promise blowing my phone up. I'm headed to Publix on to get the birthday cake," I responded back.

"I'm on my way to you right this second. DO NOT MOVE from the parking lot," Coia demanded. I was confused. Then it hit me. My dad had probably had a heart attack. His heart finally gave in, and this was it. I felt awful. We knew that he was sick, but not this bad.

"Coia, you there? Is it Daddy? Is he okay?"

As I went to pick up my purse to head in to Publix, I peeked at the text message Dereck sent me.

You're my favorite person! (heart) emoji!

I wish I could have reacted, but I had to see about my dad. In my peripheral vision, I saw a midnight-blue Tahoe rush around the parking lot, running over the curb. It was Coia driving like a bat out of hell.

"Girl, what the fu…" I could not get the words out.

"Celeste, something happened at the twins' school. It's all over the fucking news. No one has been able to reach you!" Coia described as she screamed the words.

"What? When? My babies' school?" I asked, confused.

Coia could not give me a straight answer; she was in panic mode. Now, so was I. She did not have to say where we were going. My phone continued to ring, nonstop. Now, I know why.

"Coia, take the back way. There is a shortcut!" I screamed in panic mode. She turned on the radio, and my worst nightmare as a teacher and a mother came true.

"Today events are unfolding where a gunman has gone into Elite Success Academy, an elementary private school, on a rampage and shot several office staff. No word as of yet if he shot any of the elementary students. So far seven people have been killed."

My heart. My heart, my chest hurt so much. I felt as if an air-bag had deployed and knocked the absolute life out of my body. I couldn't breathe. It hurt so bad. I hurt so bad. My babies were in danger while I was out on a sexual escapade. I doubled over in the car in panic. The ride to the school seemed like three hours. I couldn't answer my phone. Coia tried talking to me to calm me down. "I'm sure the kids are okay. They probably just shot the front office people. No one would hurt babies, no person could be that awful," she said convincingly.

We approached the rear of the school. My eyes scanned everything within my sight: crowded streets, teachers, parents crying, running toward the policed area. I could not focus because my mind was calculating a thousand things at one time.

Yellow perimeter tape surrounded every entrance of the school.

As we got closer to the school, my heart felt like it was going to burst outside my rib cage. There had to be at least twenty rescue trucks and twice that many police officers guiding people and walking groups of students to designated areas of the school. Waves of people were all over the place running back and forth. Some of those people worked at the school; others were frantic parents just like me. Chaos was EVERYWHERE! My legs were shaking uncontrollably, not like they had been earlier that day. Fear attacked me.

"I can't get any closer," Coia said.

I didn't have even a second to respond. I grabbed the handle of her door and jumped out of the truck even as Coia was still moving. Running past a long row of cars, I just felt sick immediately to my stomach. I trotted up a hill past four houses that were in close proximity to the school. The roads were congested with traffic as desperate parents tried to find their children. Cars were parked illegally all over grass and blocking business entrances as parents searched for their kids. I ran with heels on my feet, no purse in hand, yelling to no one in particular, "Mia, Nia! Mia, Nia!"

"Mommy is coming," I said to my daughters even though I knew they could not hear me at the time.

The more I ran, the more people I saw running. The terror had really set in, and I was more afraid than I had ever been in my life, more afraid than that night behind the beauty shop. I had to push to get through the crowd. Parents were holding each other, crying and waiting to hear what was going on in the school. Others were screaming their children's names, trying to get their attention. Directly across the street was a two-story home, stucco home. Students and teachers were gathered there also. I thought I would try my luck there since the school parking lot was so crowded.

"Excuse me, have you, by any chance, seen my daughters, Mialondra and Nialonda Thomas? They are twins. Is it possible that they ran over here with an adult in all of the pandemonium?" I asked in desperation.

A man and a woman were sniffling and crying uncontrollably while hugging a little blond boy with wild curly hair. He was missing a shoe and had stains of maroon and red all over his Oshkosh jumper. He looked like he was in shock. I heard him say to his parents, "I was brave, Mommy, I did not cry. I did just what the teacher told me to do."

All I could think of was, *How lucky they are to at least they have their son.* I was jealous over something so simple. No one had acknowledged my question, and I was still without my girls. I ran back to the end of the driveway and overheard another first grader giving his account of what happened. "A man shot my teacher, he hurt my friends," and he broke down in tears. That upset me so much. His dad picked him up and hugged him firmly while cupping the back of his little head. Finally, the mother of the little blond boy slowly turned her head my way, acknowledging that she heard my question.

"We have not seen a Mia or Nia over here," she stated. Oh god, that was Carter's mom. I remembered her from the Christmas play. She made the best almond crescent cookies. I overheard a few voices say to no one in particular that Ms. Nicholas had not emerged from the chaos. None of the other teachers or students had seen her yet. I almost fainted. "That was Mia's teacher. God, help me find my baby."

"The PE teacher just happened to be able to scoop a few of the kids out of the hall while everything was happening. He took a side door through the cafeteria and got them here safely," a middle-aged gentleman added.

Five minutes had passed. It was the longest five minutes ever. A lady that had been reunited with her son came up to me. She had been crying; her face was blushed and pink, eyes swollen and red. Before I could ask anything, a little voice said, "Hi, Mia's mom." I looked at the little one; he was Noah and had been transferred into Mia's class about two months ago. Unsure of what to say to a six-year-old that had been through such tragedy, I responded to Noah, "Awwww, hello, sweetheart!"

"Noah, did you see either Mia or Nia when the PE teacher brought you over here, honey?" his mom asked.

Noah's father came up as we were talking and picked him up just before he could answer. His mother immediately embraced her husband. "He's okay, honey, he's okay," she said in between sobs. I was standing there, looking alone and hopeless.

"I did not see the twins anywhere. It was so noisy," Noah turned and said to me in a tearful little voice.

Noah, his mother, and his father all cried in relief. I joined them in tears. I felt a hand grab me; it was Promise.

"Prom—" I could not get his whole name out before I lost it! I bawled as if I had not seen him in years.

I hugged him out of fear, obligation, and comfort. He knew this was a horrible sign. I was alone without either of the girls. My makeup was gone; my hair was wild and wiry. Normally, he would tease me or say some smart shit. He was just as worried as I was.

He looked at me with the saddest look I had ever seen on his face. "C, I got here fast as I could. Have you heard anything about the girls yet?"

"Promise, I…I can't find them."

"I came over here praying just maybe they ran over here for help…" I felt like my legs were growing limp and could not hold the weight of my body any longer.

Promise grabbed me up quickly. "Pull it together, C, I need you to keep me strong. Come on, we gotta find our babies. We ain't got time for this right now."

I wanted to be offended that he was not more supportive, but he was right. I needed to pull it together and find my damn kids.

I steadied myself, dried my face with the mint-green blazer I was wearing, and tossed my hair out of my face.

Promise and I ran back across the street to the main parking lot of the school where all hell was breaking loose. It was confusing where to even start looking amid the mayhem. We were all scurrying around like mice, trying to find our kids. Amid the craziness, the words were reiterated throughout the crowd, "Someone shot the principal and two teachers!" Dread took over my legs once again, as Promise hurried me through the crowd. I had to take a deep breath. I rested my body against the side of a news van that had been there since my arrival. I held my head down in a silent prayer. I did not need Marcus hurrying me because I needed to talk to God at that moment, against the van.

God, I have not been the most humble or the best Christian. I realize that I need a lot of work, but, Father, God, I know you can do all things! Today, right now please give me a sign that my girls are safe and sound. Please, God, I need this. Please don't let my babies pay for all of my sins and mistakes.

As soon as I lifted my head from prayer, I saw Nia's teacher, and a huge wave of relief and fear seized me all at once. I ran to her. Before I could hug Mrs. Rodriquez, Nia's little head popped out from behind her long skirt. She was walking with four to five other first graders all trying to find their parents. Mrs. Rodriguez was visibly dismayed, saying, "They were so brave, they were so brave…" She collapsed right there on the sidewalk. The babies surrounded her and cried along with her. The look on her face said it all! I could not form words. I picked Nia up so fast.

"Niaaaaaaa, my baby. I was so scared, pumpkin," I blubbered.

"Mommy, Mommy, I was looking for you!" she belted out in the sweetest voice. I had never been so excited to hear her call me that.

"We had to lay down under the tables in the chorus room and be really quiet," Nia carried on. "I was so scared," Nia repeated and started crying.

Promise, equally overcome with emotion, grabbed Nia out of my hands and hugged her as tightly as he could. "My baby girl, my girl…Daddy's girl. Don't scare Daddy like that again. I could not live without my baby girl, you know that?"

Nia hugged her daddy back.

"I wish you were there, Daddy, to fight that bad man with the gun," she said to her father with sobs and tears.

"Damn right, Daddy would have knocked the hell out of that mutha—" Promise said to her right before I interjected, "Promise, we gotta find Mia."

We had a conversation as if we were in the middle of my living room.

"Baby girl, did you see your sister, Mia, while y'all were coming down the hall?" Nia responded with her head shaking no from side to side.

Promise then asked, "Did you see her while y'all were hiding under the table?" Nia repeated the head-shake no.

He was trying to keep me and Nia calm. That same fear hit me as if the entire situation of the school shooting was brand-new to me. I was still missing a child. At that moment, I was so angry with myself for not allowing the girls to be in the same class together. "I thought it would hinder their individuality." How fucking stupid! Now I'm looking for my other baby. Fear and anxiety crept back into my legs and throat. It hurt so much. Just to breathe hurt.

"Mia!" I screamed.

Promise continued hugging Nia as I began combing through the crowd again

"Mia, baby, where are you?" I screamed at least twenty times.

I walked up a slight hill to a tent in the middle of the parking lot with familiar faces who worked for the school and at least a dozen police officers. As I approached, I saw several parents holding each other, crying at the same time. They were all headed to a middle school that was very close in proximity; the police called it the safe zone.

I saw a familiar face, the librarian. I remember her from the book fair last year. She was a nice lady.

"Please tell me there is a chance that you saw Mia," I questioned.

Immediately she turned around in the direction of the school where we had just left and answered, "We both saw a little girl with caramel skin, wiry ponytails, red ribbon, and her school uniform." I left the librarian right there and sprinted like a track star. I ran up behind my baby.

"Mialondra," I called desperately. The little girl turned around, and it was not her. The deflation I felt. I was angry; why would she say some shit like that? The librarian was the typical white lady that thinks all Black kids look alike. I was desperate. It was not the librarian's fault.

"Mia, Mia, where are you?" I screamed louder.

The crowd thinned out just a little. Some families reunited and drove their kids home. There were news cameras EVERYWHERE! They were trying to interview anyone who would take the invite. I saw a couple holding their daughter in a tearful appreciation for the teacher who lost her life to save their daughter, giving a detailed account of their experience to the newswoman standing along the perimeter tape.

I envied the news lady. When this story is over, she will go home and have dinner with her family and move on to the next story tomorrow. But me, I couldn't find my daughter, and it felt horrible! Sequoia had caught up with me once more with no child in her possession.

"Celeste, maybe she is in another holding area. Don't worry. We will find her," she assured me.

It was getting later in the afternoon; the remaining parents became more anxious and unnerved about what was going on. I texted Promise to update him on Mia. We agreed to meet back at the tent in the parking lot.

I felt like throwing up. I felt a pain in my chest that I could not put into words, yet I had to keep looking for my baby.

"I can't understand why they won't release the rest of the kids," Promise argued in an irate tone.

The police chief asked if the remaining parents would move to the large red portables at the rear of the school so they could get the last few kids reunited with their families. Sequoia and I both complied with no hesitation.

"Hell, no, you can reunite me with my daughter right damn here, right fucking now. We been waiting out here for three hours, and I'm not moving to another damn spot! Where is my daughter?" Promise asked.

The police chief tried to calm him down with a sincere "I understand, sir. This is the most difficult thing we have ever had to do in our line of duty. We want to find your daughter as much as you want her found."

Promise, with reservation, followed the directive and walked over to the portable behind the PE field. The portable was a big red building with chipped wood on the outside. It was obvious that this building was not used very often the way chairs and tables were pushed against the walls. I hate the color red. I just hate it!

Among the crowd, I heard the most disturbing news; parents were on the floor crying in groups, supporting one another while it was said that one entire class was missing, including the teacher. In order to not faint right there, I told myself that it had to be misinformation. Another overwhelmed parent came to me and asked what class my child was in. Once I said "Mrs. Nicholas," she looked at me strangely.

"My son was in the class next to Mrs. Nicholas. I'm so scared because I have not seen any of the kids in his class," she said, mixed with tears.

I did not know her, but I held her anyway. We shared the same terror and grief.

"Parents, can I have your attention, please. I need for you all to come back to the rear of the firehouse," the police chief bellowed.

Outraged and apprehensive parents asked why. Three hours and forty families later, it was obvious why we were in that back portable. The news of our children was not good.

The police chief muffled through the rest of his impromptu speech, "This is now a recovery effort. I regret to inform you all that no more children will be coming out. Twenty-three of our students were shot. The students in Mrs. Nicholas's class as well as Mr. Wilson's class are no longer with us. Both of those brave teachers died shielding their students."

It did not register at first what was happening.

I looked at Promise and Coia. "Is he saying our kids are not coming home with us? Mia is gone?" I asked them both in denial. "Is that what he said?" I asked to be sure.

I screamed so loud that I drowned out the choral screams of the other grieving parents. It was the most horrific, helpless feeling in the world. I had never seen Promise cry before. This sad day, he bawled and could not hold it in. Just the sounds coming out of that portable were heart-wrenching. We all cried long, painful moans.

That moment would forever be etched in my mind as the worst day of my life.

I ran to the opening of the back portable door to "throw up" over the edge. I let everything on the inside of me out. In my head, I yelled at every parent who reunited with their kids leaving us to mourn. Why couldn't I take my Mia home? As cruel as it sounded, I wanted to trade places with any of those parents who had found their kid. Those families were now nestled in their safe home while we carried the heavy load of grief. I cried and clutched my chest at the same time because I surely thought my heart was going to exit my chest at that moment. I wanted to die! I hurt so much. I just knew this had to be a mistake.

In my mind, Mia was going to bust in that portable and ask me, "Momma, why are all of y'all in here crying like this?"

She didn't come through the door. In fact, her little body was lying in the halls of Elite Success Academy like garbage on the floor. She only weighed forty-eight pounds. Who needed an assault gun to kill a first grader?

I screamed her name; I don't know why.

"Mia, I'm sorry, baby. It's your birthday."

"Mia, please. This can't be real."

Promise picked my slumped body off the back portable steps and carried me to his car. Sequoia shielded her tears from Nia. She followed us while holding Nia's hand.

THE NEXT DAY

I woke up feeling sick in Promise's bed. It was surreal. None of this was happening. I knew that Mia and Nia would come jump in Promise's bed and disturb my sleep with conversation of school and baby dolls at any minute. Nia was asleep beside me, but there was no Mia. I cried quietly and went looking for her. I walked in the living room where Promise was with swollen red eyes. He was talking to his parents and my mom. When they saw me, all conversation stopped. They all looked at me like a crumpled piece of paper about to blow away in the wind. They just knew I was going to fall apart any minute.

They were right. "Promise, where is Mia?" I probed.

"Celeste, do you want some coffee?" Mama asked.

"No, I just want to go out and look for Mia, that's all I want," I demanded once more.

My momma just grabbed my daddy and buried her head in his chest with huge sobs. My daddy had dementia; he had no idea what was going on. Promise tried to get me to go back to bed. He looked at me but struggled to get words out of his mouth.

"C, Mia not coming back, baby, she just not," Promise affirmed with a shaky voice. He held his head down in his hands as tears rolled down his face.

"Mia!" I screamed out in crushing pain. I thought if I called her enough, maybe she would answer. I could do nothing else but call her name.

Part of me thought she would answer.

Both of Promise's parents were crazy about the twins. When we first had them, they volunteered the first month to babysit to give us

138

both a break. This worked out fine, until all the fighting and cheating made things difficult for us all.

His parents went into his room just to see if Nia had awakened. But no one could answer my question. A mental picture of the school with all the police and rescue trucks haunted me. I opened my purse looking for my cell. I had not seen my phone for the past eighteen hours. I had hoped Mia had it, playing around somewhere, hiding from me. I scanned my phone closely, hoping someone found Mia hiding across the street or in a supply closet and called me. When I looked at my phone, I saw twenty-two missed calls from work, friends, and neighbors. I threw my phone clear across the room.

As my phone crashed against the wall, I saw where Promise had two large birthday presents in the corner of his living room. There were balloons that read, "Happy birthday to my favorite girls." They had Black Barbie designs all over them with streams of Barbie ribbon going across the ceiling. Promise didn't do all this. One of his skanks must have tried to score bonus points and arranged this, probably Ms. Angie. I could not, would not celebrate ever again!

The seventy-five-inch television in the living room displayed the school shooting like a bad movie.

"The gunman was twenty-one-year-old Francis 'Frank' Fernsby. He entered the front of Elite Success Academy Charter School and shot the assistant principal, who tried to deny him entry, the principal, and the secretary who was sitting at the front desk with an AR15 assault rifle. He then proceeded down the hall, where he shot three teachers, a security guard, and twenty-two first-grade students. He took his own life as he heard police approaching the school. The students and staff killed will be forever remembered by this very tragic event. Right now there is no word on the motive of the killer. The body was discovered among two of the students that he slaughtered near a janitor's closet.

"The sheriff's office will be holding a press conference at five to give an update on the tragedy at ESA Charter School. Back to you, Patti."

It had been one day since my life turned inside out. This story was headlined every news station, both local and national. I saw the girls' school on CNN. How did this happen?

That's all I know about the animal who used a weapon of war and killed my baby. Did he hate his father, mother, or teachers? Why would even the most demented person hurt babies? Oh my god, my baby must have suffered terribly. Just when I thought I was all out of tears, my eyes swelled up and I started a river of tears all over again. As I started my refreshed meltdown, I heard the anger rise up in my parents' voices.

"Why the hell would a coward go hurt those poor innocent babies?" my mom wailed.

Right after the news excerpt, Promise ran outside to be alone. We all knew he had been crying, but he still did not want us to see him like that. The roar of pain that came after that was nothing I had ever heard before. My dad and his dad ran after him to make sure he was okay.

"God, please tell me this is not real," I begged. I paced back into Promise's room with Nia and just lay there in a bucket of my own tears, trying not to wake her. Have you ever tried to cry silently? Do you know how hard that is? I haven't even thought about what I am going to tell her about her sister or yesterday's events.

I wanted to die. It felt as though Francis Frank whatever reached into my chest with his bare hands and ripped my heart out of my rib cage. This had to be what a heart attack felt like.

The doorbell rang; there were people from all over Promise's neighborhood there to give condolences. They hugged him and kissed his cheek while he thanked them for coming by. I could not pull myself out of bed to go be social with anyone. I wanted to lie down beside Nia and never move out of that spot again.

"Celeste, baby, you have to eat something," my mom indicated a she gently touched by back and rubbed my arm.

"I don't want to eat, I don't want to drink. Just let me die," I said in overwhelming grief.

"Okay, let's go with that… If you die, what happens to Nia? Do you think she deserves to lose her mother and her sister?" my mom pointed out with anger.

Promise looked mortified. "The hospital just called and wants one of us to identify—" He barely got it out. Promise broke down and collapsed in my lap. Shit, I didn't know how we were going to pull it together. I had never seen this man cry, ever!

"It's not supposed to be like this! Parents should not have to bury their kids, especially seven-year-old kids!" my daddy yelled.

Promise's parents had the awful task of identifying my seven-year-old daughter. I could not move. The last thing I wanted to see was the type of harm done to my baby girl at the hands of a monster. All our cell phones were ringing one after the other. I think people wanted to know if all this was real. Did Mia really die?

*****

In all the pain and grief, I let myself surrender to a fraction of sleep. I was so tired but sick on the inside. Hours later, I was still in bed. I had on the same clothes from the previous day. I had been reminded all morning that I had not eaten, bathed, moved, nothing. The news reporters were camped out at my house; I refused to go home and go through that. I know Mrs. Jackson was really entertained by my tragedy. She wanted to be in my business so bad. She was probably giving news interviews and tours of my house. Even if I wanted to, I could not hide this ghastly horror from the world.

I could faintly hear Nia talking to Coia and her grandmother. She didn't sound like she was crying. In fact, she sounded normal. How could she be normal after all that?

"Grandma, my teacher took us to a room by the gym and made us get in a big closet. We played *Quiet Mouse*. None of us could make any noise, she said."

My mom asked other probing questions, "Did you see the bad man with a gun?"

"No, Grandma, but we heard firecrackers and loud fireworks with people screaming!" she added.

"Kids were crying, and that's when the teacher told us to play Quiet Mouse for candy," Nia stated. I heard her say they had to all sneak into a big closet in the music class.

"We just sat on the floor in the music room. My teacher put a desk in front of the door so nobody could get in. We heard a lot of fireworks and screaming," Nia emphasized.

I did not think it was a great idea to have her talk about the shooting, but maybe she needed to get it out. I did not want to hear any more about it.

THE FUNERAL

Friday afternoon was the first time I was able to see Mia since sh...
I still couldn't say it. It was the wake, and I had to get Mia's favorite dress. I let Nia pick it out. She still thinks her sister is going to
come back. Nia even went to get her sister's favorite doll, Hanna. She
insisted that Mia would want to sleep with her doll. I guess we had
to get Hanna an outfit to match as well.

Coia, Jennifer, and Nikki took me purchase the dress. The dress
was a pastel yellow. It had crinoline underneath, lace over the puffy
sleeves, and the most beautiful roses trimmed around the edges of
the dress.

It was a really quick exchange and the first time I loathed
shopping.

We arrived at the funeral home and to meet the rest of my family. I collected the shoes, dress, and Hanna out of the car. I handed
the dress over to a lady I didn't know, but she worked for the funeral
home. My stomach was in knots. The gunman had shot my baby
three times, once in her little head and twice in her torso with an
assault weapon. It tore her little body almost in half. Part of her skull
on the left side was missing. All the makeup and lace hats in the
world were not enough to cover the evil done to my daughter at
the hands of an inhumane dog. A closed-casket funeral was the only
option. I fainted right there in the funeral home. The only thing I
remember was Promise and my brother carrying me over to a padded
pew. I released it all to Promise. "Mama, I gotta get out of here. I
can't do this. I am not that mother on TV who stares at the casket for
hours, forgives the shooter, and puts a brave face on for the public," I
said to her and the rest of the family standing around me. They were

walking on eggshells, not wanting to say the wrong thing. Coia drove me home.

The rest of the family sprinkled in one at a time.

The funeral was tomorrow, and I couldn't face family, the media, or nosy-ass people who just wanted to see how broken I was. I gathered every single prescription I had in my room. There were at least seven pills in my hand of various colors, white, orange, oval shape, blue, and some strange large yellow one. With a glass of Seagram's Gin, I swallowed every one of those seven pills. I really attempted suicide. Promise found on the floor, after tapping me to wake up, he knew something was wrong. He called a paramedic friend who pumped my stomach right there on-site. Promise cursed me out. I was on the bathroom floor.

"C, what the fuck wrong with you, man? How is this going to solve any fucking thing? You can't be this damn stupid to kill yourself. This is the most selfish shit you've ever done," he said in tears.

After I threw up a few times all over the floor, I was conscious. He got down on his knees, and we cried together.

*****

I could smell bacon cooking. The aroma of homemade biscuits and bacon filled my entire home. My stomach growled, but I had no appetite at all. I had been out since 5:00 p.m. the previous day. I was being monitored around the clock by family and friends.

"I want to tell you good morning, baby, but it's nothing good about it, Celeste," my mama said as she sat beside me on the bed.

I was in the bed, but I wasn't sleep. I tried to end it all yesterday so that I would not have to face another day, but I failed at that too.

Today was Mia's funeral, and I have been dreading it for four very long days. I fucking hate funerals, period!

It's so awful for a parent to have to bury their child, a seven-year-old. It's the cruelest event life could ever dish out. "It's nine o'clock, baby, you have got to get out of bed and try to start getting dressed. I turned on the flat iron for you."

It took seven entire minutes for me to actually form words and make them come out of my mouth. "Mama, I'm not going to no funeral. I'm not saying goodbye to Mialondra, not today or any other day." I then put the covers over my head with tears running down the left side of my face on to my pillow. In college we had to read Elisabeth Kubler-Ross's stages of grief. I don't know where I fell in any of the five stages, but it had to be a mixture of anger and denial.

Promise barged in the room and asked my mama to give him a second. Coia came in right behind him looking helpless.

"Celeste, do you think this is easy for me? Do you think this is easy for your mother?" he asked with a combination of grief and irritation. "Come on, baby, do this for Nia. She is so confused in all of this," he continued.

The words hit me like two center blocks in the stomach. "Nia, I'm so sorry. I can't stop crying, I want to… I just can't. It hurts too bad.

Coia went into my closet and found a black chiffon dress with a horizontal ruffle down the back side. She must have purchased it. I had never seen that dress before. I did not want to go, and I certainly did not care about what I put on. I still don't know how Nikki did my hair, put on my makeup, or help me into the dress. As I peeped from under my black mesh funeral hat masking my tears, I saw a line of cars so far down the street that the procession had to be miles long. A television crew was parked outside my home, and I felt so violated. I was at my most vulnerable at this moment, and news cameras were flashing, trying to take it all in. I wondered if the parents of the other slain children went through this. As we rode in the family car, the vision of the tiny, little pink casket was imprinted in my brain for life. It was a tiny, little pink casket with a vine of flowers that aligned the side. It's just not natural to have a casket for a person this little.

We lined up outside the church. I remember Coia putting a white pill under my tongue with a quick squirt of water to wash it down. Jennifer and Nikki surrounded me like a fence.

I walked to the front row, staring directly at her casket with her picture on top. She looked so happy in that picture. It was the third week of school, and she insisted on wearing a bright-green bow that didn't match a thing she had on. I begged that girl to change her bow. She was a willful little thing. I never understood sitting the family right in front of the casket. It is horrifying; it's torture. Who thought this process was a good idea?

Choir sang a sad song, I looked behind me, and the churched was filled with standing room only: teachers who survived the shooting, parents, my school staff. Keith? Why did he come? I could not even elaborate on that thought. Kade was two rows behind me with dark shades. He loved Mia. That was his little partner in crime.

As I stared at the casket cradling my baby girl, my mind faded off to the day that Mia picked the doll out of the store, Hannah. It was a little white doll, but it's what she wanted. I tried so hard to convince her to get a doll that looked like her, but Hannah was who she wanted. She told me all dolls were pretty, white or black. I was at the cash register about to pay for the doll, and she walked away from me. Nia did not move far away at all. Mia thought it would be a fun game to hide in the clothes rack where I could not find her. I had Hannah draped across my left arm, and Nia had her doll. I called for Mia, and she did not answer. Nia called for her sister, and she did not answer. I was so scared. The panic that passed through my body that day could not compare to the pain I felt at this moment. The clothes, makeup, and her beautiful hair may have covered a lot, but it couldn't cover the right side of her missing skull. The truth is, a demonic, twisted asshole who probably hated his mother and father killed my fucking baby for no damn reason. Why my child, I couldn't process it.

"I leaned over to Promise. I don't know what Sequoia gave me, but I feel a little different," I said. I looked to my left and saw my Big Mama. How could I have missed her?

Beside me, Promise had on shades. He looked so handsome in his suit and tie. He had tears running down his face. I forgot all this time that he lost a child too. He was trying to be strong for me and Nia. "Are you going to be okay?" he asked in a whisper.

"I got you," he confirmed and grabbed my hand. Several people had gotten up and spoken of the tragedy, the undeserving death of a seven-year-old, and God's plan. It angered me, and I had to say something.

I felt myself get up. Promise was trying to hold me in my seat without making a scene. It did not work. The church became silent as they saw me rise and walk to the microphone. No one expected the grieving mother to speak, not even the grieving mother.

I sniffed and wiped my nose before speaking. "Thank you all for coming to support my angel…" The tears started rolling once again. I could barely get the words out.

"I can't understand this agonizing tragedy. I feel like I am living a nightmare, and it won't go away. Many of you have given your spiritual point of view to make sense of this horrible incident. But, you can't make sense of this. This is very new for me, and the hurt is indescribable. I ask you all to please approach me with caution and that you think before you speak. *I DO NOT want to hear 'It was all part of God's plan' or 'She's in a better place.' What god would have a seven-year-old die is this manner? What god would snatch a first grader from her mother, twin sister, and family?* If you think my words are harsh, I understand. But, I mean this sincerely: do not utter those words to me or anything like them. Those things make YOU feel better, not me!"

The church was so silent after I spoke. The pastor was at a loss of words.

I looked over to the right and stared at the picture of my beautiful Mia on top of her closed casket. And I broke down as if it were only me and Mia in the church. "Mia, I'm so sorry I wasn't there for you." I wept loudly. Promise came up beside me to assist me to my seat. "Celeste, come on, that's enough, baby, they get it," he said.

I stretched out my arms so that I could caress her picture. I could not rub her face anymore; all I had was the picture. The more I cried, the more the church erupted in tears. It was the saddest thing. The preacher looked at me as he took the microphone, and he told me not to lose faith. "Sister Belle, just know that God will cover you. It may not make sense—there is nothing I can say to make logic out of this. I do know that God loves you."

I heard him but did not really hear him. I was so glad when it was all over. I don't know what Coia gave me, but it got me through.

I was so overtaken by grief I had not noticed that Coia stood beside me, holding me as I spoke to the church. I love my best friend. She was just as devastated as I was. Lord knows she was always trying to save Mia from getting into trouble. They were true partners in crime.

The funeral ended. As I saw the hearse leave with my daughter, I knew it would be the last time that I would see her. Promise followed my absolute request to not allow the burial at the graveyard. I was NOT, under any circumstance, going to allow anyone to lower my baby in the ground, hell no! I did have control over that. Sequoia came over and put her head on my shoulder. She was just as torn up as I was. In all this, I forgot that she needed to grieve also. I loved my best friend and all her craziness.

SEQUOIA

The repass was at my mother's house. Nikki and Jennifer helped set everything up. It was getting late, and people were starting to depart. I saw Nikki picking up plates and taking them to the kitchen. There was awkward silence. Sequoia finally broke it.

"Okay, y'all ready?" she asked us. Jennifer was still holding my hand, while Nikki continued collecting dishes from all over the house. We were all gathered in the living room. Most of the crowd had left my parents' house after Mia's funeral. It had been the longest day in the world, but of course, my girls would never leave me on a day like this. Sequoia was about to turn it all the way up, and I needed the distraction. Without fail, Coia went right into her narrative. She must have been bursting at the seams, holding this shit in.

"*So*, I was in a restaurant and saw Dre with a random chick. Okay, no big deal, right? He spoke. I spoke, 'No hard feelings.' I wasn't even petty and let her know he just ate my pussy last week after he dropped our son off. So the random ho stepped out of pocket and says to him, 'You got five minutes to find us a table or you gone be here by yourself. I don't do tired-ass baby mamas.' I let that shit slide because I was in a good headspace. I just smiled and gave the waitress my to-go order. This bitch could not leave it alone and says, 'She don't look better than me anyway.'" Everyone in the room paused. Nikki stopped cleaning, and Jennifer sat down on the sofa. We knew what was coming next, Hurricane Sequoia.

"That was when I let that 'five-dollar jewelry-selling-ass bitch' get it. I grabbed a side dish of marinara sauce on the table next to me and dashed that shit right in her motherfucking eyes. The manager came over and grabbed me, leaving her in a position to hit me. Of

149

course, I felt threatened, so I smashed his ass with the small bowl that the sauce was in. He should not have touched me." The room was silent. We all stared at Coia with bewilderment. Coia has done some crazy shit, but this sounded like it was headed south. I turned my head sideways and repeated the words "marinara sauce." Those were the first words I said since we left the church. Sequoia continued her story, "The police got there immediately. Those assholes put me in the back of the police car for two fucking hours. Dre stayed all two hours explaining to the manager that I was under tremendous stress, pleading for him not to press charges. They finally let me out of the car. Ooh, that pissed the bitch off! If I wasn't so infuriated, I could have found humor looking at that chipped-tooth, smoky-bones-ass bitch. She had red sauce all over her face and in that uuuugly [really extended the word unnecessarily] -ass blond synthetic wig. I followed her ass to the rear of the restaurant, pointed two fingers out, and quoted the *Color Purple* on her ass, 'Until you do right and get a human hair wig, bitch, EVERYTHING you do gone fail.' She walked away mad as fuck! Not only did Dre plead my case, but he totally forgot she was there. Muthafucka, I'm the mother of his son, that's what the fuck he's supposed to do. I have always held Dre down, since Daytona Beach-week days! He know. You know what, y'all? I didn't even know dirty footdragger's name."

We had so many questions but could not get a word in, not even Nikki. All it took was one thing for us to focus on, just one. In this case, we couldn't let the "chipped tooth" comment go. So as Jennifer tried to interject with a question, Coia responded, "I ain't finished." She continued.

"The manager finally agreed to dismiss the charges and had the unmitigated gall to require me to sign a statement saying that I would not come within fifty feet of their establishment ever! I did sign the shit 'cause I ain't wanna go to jail! But, I went to the entrance of that raggedy shit, bent all the way over, lifted up my damn dress, and told that bastard to kiss the crack of my black ass. I will never go back to that shit, and y'all don't need to go either! If y'all love me, you will not patronize that place ever again."

All three of us burst out laughing.

After that entire soliloquy, Coia requested that we not "patronize" this restaurant. That shit was *so* funny to me. I mean, although I didn't want to laugh, I could not help but think this bitch is crazy!

Promise came in and found us all laughing at once. He knew it had to be Coia related. He found a seat next to Sequoia and put his head on her shoulder. Never in a million years did I think Sequoia and Promise would ever get along. They had been feuding since college.

Promise and I met my first year of college and his second year of college at University of South Florida. He did not notice me at first. Promise was a brain and completely focused on his books, while I was more occupied by being free from parents and partying. He was balancing basketball and class. We started studying together. He was scrawny and skinny at first. During his senior year, he transformed. Over the summer, he lifted weights and became bulky and muscular. His face went from naked and skinny to defined with a full beard. All the girls began to notice. We started dating. Promise was my first. We dated for a while, then the cheating started. By my senior year, I was pregnant with twins. The delivery was rough. Promise had a big game that night. His parents were in the delivery room instead of him. That pissed Sequoia off.

"Who gives a shit if he has a game tonight? His babies are being born. That's the damn priority," she spouted. She said this as I was pushing the babies out. His parents were right outside the delivery room. My mama was on the other side and did not make it much better. So they were bashing him while I was pushing. Mia came out fine. Nia had a cord wrapped around her neck. That was when Promise walked in the room. He and Coia traded places. She looked at him like he had stolen money out of her bank account. She was livid with him.

"'Bout time you got here," she said with attitude.

"Mind your damn business, man," he responded back to Coia curtly.

After two long hours, they were able to get the cord from around Nia's neck and out of the womb. I took them home a few days later. I was resting in a chair when Coia came to my parents' house in an uproar. She tried to tell me the story calmly without waking the babies. "I just saw Promise in the mall with another girl. It was some bitch in a sorority. That nigga knew I saw him. He tried to hide by ducking into a store when I looked in his direction. He gave his self away. He didn't have no damn business in Home Goods," she preached. Coia continued with the story.

"The girl looked like a little freshman in a blue bongo skirt and vest. Don't worry, I walked up to his sorry ass and threw my damn lemonade in his face. I paid three dollars for that Chik-fil-A lemonade!" she exclaimed. They both tried to act all shocked.

"While my best friend is at home with your two newborn daughters, you are out here hoeing around. Tell your li'l trick that you got a woman and a whole damn family," she proclaimed.

"I caused a big-ass scene," she added. I was devastated. I knew he cheated, but he became ridiculous with it. That day, he told me he was at work. Coia was right there to wipe my tears. She hated his ass for that shit. I hated him for it too. She had even come up with an elaborate plan of revenge to get his ass back for cheating. The plan was for me to invite him over as if nothing happened. Sequoia went to the store and got chocolate chip cookie mix and ex-lax chocolates. She came back to the house and watched the babies while I mixed the ingredients. I added the eggs, butter, and mixture. The last ingredient was the ex-lax. I made sure to put enough in them to take his ass out for the day. So I baked them and I baked a noncontaminated batch so I would not look suspicious. Promise came over to give me some money for the twins.

He walked in feeling guilty. Instead of giving me eye contact, he washed his hands and went to living room to pick up the babies one at a time. I pretended as if nothing had happened. He was trying to feel me out and see what Coia told me. I acted as if everything was fine.

"Hey, I was craving some cookies and just made a fresh batch," I said while eating a cookie.

He looked confused, like, why wasn't I mad? That should have been his first damn clue. I took a plate over with four or five cookies. I handed him a bottle of water and started cooing at the twins.

Promise went along with it. He ate the first cookie. "Umm, these are good, and they are warm," he said while eating another one. He took a swallow of water and at the other two.

He only stayed for a little while. He kissed the babies, then he kissed me goodbye. A couple of hours had gone by, and I wondered if the cookies worked. The phone rang. It was Promise. "What the fuck you put in those cookies? Man, I almost shitted on myself at work. I been to the bathroom four times. I'm calling you from the bathroom right now," he blubbered. I laughed my ass off on the other end of the phone.

"I don't know. I was fine," I commented while holding back laughter.

I called Coia and let her know it worked. She thought it was hilarious. This was our life for many years. Now they were sitting beside each other like they were besties. Mia's death brought them together and ended the ten-year feud of Promise and Sequoia, at least temporarily.

I dozed off. I woke up and saw Big Mama was sitting beside my bed.

"Hey, baby, did not want to alarm you. I just wanted to make sure you rest soundly," she said, stroking my hair.

I laid my head on her leg. "Celeste, you got through the hardest part. I will help you get through the rest. Drink this hot tea," she said while handing me a teacup. "It's going to help you sleep. When you get a little better, I need you to take a couple of days and come out to the country with me," she insisted. How could I say no?

ANGEL

In the dead of the night, I rose like a woman possessed, eyes wide open, body unwilling and no conscious thoughts of my own. My ears echoed the words "It's time. Now is the time." I sat straight up in the bed, perfect posture and all. My feet touched the floor. Before I could think about what was happening, it was like an invisible hand was pulling me forward. I was too unaware to be afraid. Operating in total darkness, I moved as if I were a ghost walking through the halls. Without noticing, I had gathered my work satchel, laptop, and handy tablet. Even in the middle of the night, it was habit for me to have paper and a writing utensil close. My ideas hit me at the oddest time. I must say this was one of the oddest.

As I traveled down the hall, I bumped into a box which had some of Mia's photos at the top. It was then I woke up. My beautiful baby, the little girl who challenged me to get better got my whole attention at 1:20 a.m. This time it was different. I did not cry. I did not yell or scream at God, "How could you?"

Mia, even in death, got me up out of bed.

Her little hands must have pulled me out of bed, but it was God: the same god I cursed, the same one I stopped believing in, and the same god I thought played a cruel joke to punish me. He knew I was at a breaking point for the worst. He also knew that only Mia could bring me back. I sat down on the couch to snuggle close to her photo while lying still in the dark. Strangely but calmly, the room brightened up as if a dim flashlight pointed in my direction. I squinted, confused by sleep and fatigue.

I saw it. I saw her. I couldn't be dreaming.

He sent her with little angel wings dressed in all white. Her dress was all lace. It had the cutest puffy little sleeves that skimmed down at the elbow and flowed past her little hands. Her hair...big curls and ribbon. She was a slim little thing. The dress encased her small figure and widened below the waist. It was very long. Her ruffle socks and patent leather white shoes were so pretty. As she came closer, I wanted to grab her up and hug her. Her angel wings were the most beautiful thing I had ever seen. They were the perfect size for Mia. It reminded me of the time when she and Nia were two and wanted to be an angel and the other the damn devil for Halloween; why, I don't know.

I was so elated to see her again. I had so many questions. She sat next to me on the couch surprisingly with all her attire. In a gentle little voice, she said, "Mommy, I'm okay." I lost it. All of it!

Between tears, slob, and sorrow, I managed to get out, "I'm so sorry that I let this happen to you." As a parent, it was what I felt, guilt. I made her go to that school an hour away. She wanted to stay home and be with her dad that day, but I made her go to school. I broke down once more. "Mia, I'm the worst mom ever."

Mia took her long sleeve and wiped my eyes. "Momma, don't cry. You still are great. You took us for ice cream and sang to us at night. When we were sick, you stayed home with us and gave us whatever we wanted. You did a lot, Mama. Mommy, you have to stop feeling so sad. You can't even help Nia because you won't stop crying. God told me he has special plans for you and you have to be ready. Mommy, you do want to be ready, right?" I paused for a minute to stop sobbing and gave a glance. She continued, "It didn't hurt. It felt like I was hit with a really big snowball. It was really cold. I remember being really cold in my back and legs then falling down. Ms. Nicholas jumped in front of me and screamed at the bad man, 'No, don't hurt my babies!' He was mean and didn't listen to her. He shot her. Mia's face was lethargic as she recanted the events of the shooting, all the things I wanted to know." Did she feel a lot of pain? Who tried to protect my child from this maniac? Then she got to her part. "I tried to run for the crayon closet, and I felt a lot of cold, that's all I remember. I'm okay now, Mama. God came and got me, and Ms. Nicholas stayed with all of us kids. We walked in a line to a *big* classroom. But, it was far away from our regular school. God gave us all a choice of what kind of class we wanted to go to. Jayden and Kaitlyn went to the zoo class. I went to the nursery class with lots of babies. I get to hold little babies every day, Mama. I feed them and make them laugh." Mia sounded so excited and proud of her job. "Can you believe it's babies here in heaven and God picked me to watch over them?"

Mia loves babies! "Yes, baby, I believe it." I kissed her little cheek as she leaned over to make it easy for me.

That was the whole point; she wanted to make this easier for me. We talked for at least three hours. I fell asleep with Mia lying in my lap, telling me all about the babies. She was fine. If she couldn't be with her mama, she could be with her father.

I woke up that morning about 9:00 a.m. Mia was gone. She had to go watch over the babies in heaven. A great peace had blanketed my body. Inside I still felt empty but not angry. I did allow a single tear to slide down my face, but it was more of a cleansing. Real healing would take me awhile.

I went to the twins' room. Nia was up playing quietly with her Barbie dolls, combing their hair and dressing them up. I grabbed a doll, my favorite one, Theresa, and joined her on the floor.

"Where are my pink shoes to match Theresa's dress?" I asked her.

Nia was surprised but happy. "Hey, Mama. They are right here in her car."

I laughed. All women, including Barbies, have a pair of shoes in the car. Nia went into Barbie character quick. "Okay, there's a big party tonight at the Barbie house. We have to get ready!" I sat there thinking how resilient kids are. For the last two weeks, I had been sulking, crying, hurting and didn't consider Nia lost her best friend and sister. She didn't cave in or give up. My girls were so strong. In midthought, Nia asked, "Mommy, you think Mia misses me?"

"Of course, pumpkin. You two are everything to each other," I said ardently. I was not ready to have that discussion. We played for a couple of hours. I lost track of time with Barbie parties, weddings, and fashion shows.

I was not ready to go back to work. I didn't need the sympathy stares, the sincere condolences, or the insincere concerns.

I saw my laptop beside the couch along with my tablet. As I started looking at the notes, it became clear I needed a project to keep Mia's memory alive and something productive to do with my time. I needed to create my exit plan from the school board. It's too corrupt and political. They can hire their girlfriends, wives, lovers, whoever they wanted. I didn't want any part of it.

AWAITED VISIT

We arrived in Seffner, Florida, about 6:00 p.m. in the evening. Mama drove. She pulled into Big Momma's long dirt driveway, scanning each tree and patch of grass slowly. Big Mama had the richest soil in the ground. She had trees of every sort: orange trees, lemon trees, plum trees. Florida has a unique plum tree, Japanese plum trees. They produce the sweetest nectar in all of the south. According to Big Mama, the potency they produce can raise the dead. Big Mama has NEVER had to go to a local grocery store; she has spices and herbs all over her yard.

It seemed so much more lively and mysterious since my brother and I were little. The memories flooded my mind all at once—the good, bad, and sad. The most tranquil part of her yard was the little pond she created years ago. Big Mama always told us that pond was magic. As a kid, those words were powerful. Certainly, if rainbow fish existed in my grandmother's pond, they had to be magic! One evening, when Big Mama was entertaining guests in the house, my brother and his friend Rodney, from next door, and I all raced back and forth in the yard. Rodney wanted to scare us and told us of a haunted place in the graveyard down the street. As we walked past the pond toward the graveyard, the boys began to race. I yelled to them to wait for me, but the boys raced ahead of me as I stayed behind beside the pond. A slightly tall man with a white suit and a hat appeared in the middle of the pond. I don't know how Jerald and Rodney missed this man. He was five foot eleven with a three-piece suit on along with this wide-brimmed hat to match, white. He walked across the pond and motioned his finger in the direction for me to go to him. I was petrified. I could not go to him, nor could

I run. I was terrified, but it did not stop him from getting closer to me. I could see Jerald and Rodney running at a distance ahead of me. I was too scared to even scream for help. The tall man in the white suit bent down to my level. With a stern voice, he held his arm out to block my path. "Don't you go out of this yard! You hear me?" He didn't have to worry about it because I was too scared to move anywhere. Barely breathing, I said nothing, reversed my steps, and ran as fast as I could past the pond, the trees and finally up the steps to the house. Big Mama was so mad that I flew in the house like that while she had company. "Girl, have you lost your damn mind?" I grabbed her leg, gathering her gown around her left leg, pointing toward the direction of the pond. I feared the man in the pond more than I did Big Mama's whipping that evening. She ran out of the door, and so did the other ladies who were with her. We all left the porch and sprinted down the stairs quickly. Unfortunately, we were too late. Jerald ran full speed toward us as we were leaving the yard. He was crying uncontrollably, unable to speak coherently. Big Mama was more worried than she was mad. "What's wrong, Jerald, baby? Where is Rodney?" she asked in a very concerned tone.

Jerald jumped up into her arms and flung his arms around her neck, "He dead, Big Mama."

"What, wait a minute, this boy is talking crazy," Big Mama said while instructing us to stay in the yard and hold hands. Big Mama heard a lot of commotion down the street with several cars blaring horns and blocking the street. Big Mama and another large woman with this ugly purple purse traveled toward the chaos. I knew something was wrong when I saw her drop her head, raise her hands, and stretch them out while shouting, "Lord, no, not this child! Jesus, Jesus!" The lady with the purple bag saw that Rodney had been run over by a dump truck that was leaving the graveyard. Rodney's body was split in half and was barely threaded together with a few muscles in his midsection.

One of the neighbors who was outside was in tears and, explaining to the police, said that Rodney had run in front of the truck while racing a friend and did not see the truck until it was too late. He was racing while trying to look behind at Jerald and failed to look forward. That night we both slept in Big Mama's bed. We didn't get a whipping for going to the graveyard or me for running in the house like a wild banshee. Big Mama figured we had been punished enough. She made a special tea for Jerald to sleep peacefully with no nightmares. She went outside in the dead of night with her flashlight, collected a few roots from her garden and a cup of water from the pond. She mixed some concoction with a sprinkle of sugar and vanilla flavor. Jerald took it and went right to sleep. I thought it was strange because she did not give it to me, but I was also glad I didn't have to drink nasty pond water.

I put my head in her lap. She smelled like candles and cinnamon cookies. Big Mama asked me, "Were you running earlier because you saw the accident?"

I responded, "No, ma'am. A man in a white suit and a white hat told me not to go out of the yard."

Big Ma did not seem surprised by my description and asked, "Was he a tall man standing by the pond?"

I answered, "Big Mama, he was standing in the pond, in the middle of the pond. He was walking in the water like a magician!"

Big Mama had another strange reaction. "Oh, so you met Uncle Willie. I'm sorry he frightened you, baby, but he was trying to protect you. If you had gone down that road with the boys, it would have been you to get hit by that truck, Celeste. He had to stop you, baby doll! I had a vision of something awful happening, but in my vision, I saw you were safe in the yard and Jerald was crying on the sidewalk, but he was safe."

I fell asleep in her lap as she described her brother, Uncle Willie, in the white suit.

VOODOO

"Big Mama, you home?" I yelled out. She was in the kitchen fixing my favorite sour cream pound cake. She could not come out and greet me while she was cooking. "Celeste, is that you?" she asked.

I said in a very mild voice, "Yes, ma'am." Big Momma's house was just as big as I remember. She had lit candles all over the house from the front to the back, everywhere. I had never seen a house with so many doors. She was known for practicing roots, but my mom did not speak much about it.

"Come on, I'm in the kitchen," she extended. I don't know why, but being in the comfort of her arms made me feel safe. The tears flowed down my face and on to her shoulder. With her special handkerchief, she wiped my face. That handkerchief had to be, like, fifty years old. She had that thing since my mom was a baby.

"You don't have to talk, baby, I know why you are here. I am so glad you finally decided to pay me a visit," she sympathized. "It's not the time for me to question why you never returned my calls. I know it's still very painful, Celeste. I'm going to help you get through this, don't you worry," she assured me as I collected myself. "Just follow my instructions, pumpkin!

"First, I need for you to get your luggage and go to the second room on your left. DO NOT go in any other room than the one I tell you. Second, I want you to rest tonight. Nothing else!"

It was very easy to comply with my fragile mental state. Big Mama came in the room while I was in a light sleep; she sat on the edge of the bed with a small yellow cup. It had a string hanging from the side like a tea bag. Steam and smoke were coming from the cup.

She lifted my neck and said, "Celeste, baby, I need you to drink this. Come on now, sit up a li'l bit and drink some of this."

I sat up a little groggy and put my lips to the cup. Apprehensive that the drink would be too warm, I took a sip. She wiped my lips with that same handkerchief from decades ago. Surprisingly, it was perfectly warm. I thought back to when Big Mama gave my brother a potion when his friend was hit by a dump truck. Her homemade concoction almost seemed to make him forget about what happened over night. That's exactly what I needed! I drank the entire cup. Before I could ask her what was in it, I fell completely out on the feathered pillow.

As I was dreaming, it seemed as though I was in the room with them. I could see everything. She and my mama were in a room lit with candles. But they were not alone. The ladies from her *Women's Club* were there. In my dream, I could see myself sleeping, but I was floating through the house and above my own body. The ladies lit red and black candles, chanting half of the night. They went outside to surround the pond with white candles while throwing collected herbs and spices into it. Big Mama led two incantations. I could not understand the words or the order, but I knew something significant was happening. Big Mama had a blood-soaked washcloth in her hands. I knew it was serious. The vision was disturbing, but I was genuinely unafraid because Big Mama made sure of that. Mia was running around the pond, playing in the same dress I saw the night she came to me. She looked like a beautiful angel playing at her great-mother's house.

Big Mama was very upset about what happened to Mia. She had no idea what was going on with me at work. I wish I had called her all those times that I intended to, but I got too caught up in my own selfish world. Maybe she could have talked me out of some of the bad decisions that I made. I could clearly see that same handkerchief from decades ago overflowing with my tears floating above the pond. How in the fuck did she do that shit? It was amazing to see her at work. On a wooden makeshift table, I could see three red mason jars. They had labels on them, but I could not see the writing clearly.

Those three jars represented something sinister. I was unable to see labels or its contents.

Big Momma was a wise woman; she planned this much earlier before my arrival. If she could have retaliated against anyone, it would have been Mia's shooter. That fucking coward shot himself, so he would not have to face any punishment. If I know Big Momma, she still will conjure up something that will damn his soul to a special place in hell.

The next morning, I was groggy but alert. Big Mama and my mama were sitting in the dining room, looking through old photo albums.

"Good morning, sleepyhead," Mama looked up and said to me.

"Hey, what are you two doing up so early?" I asked them.

They both were laughing and pointing at pictures. They asked me to come over to look. Most of the photos were me as a little girl and Jerald as a preteen.

"Mama, I had the strangest dream. Both of y'all were up making magic potions with other ladies. It was insane. You guys were standing around the pond, mixing herbs and spices," I continued.

"That sounds crazy! We did play cards last night. The only thing I mixed last night were some drinks, Hennessey, orange juice, bourbon, and a li'l Sprite," Big Mama said, chuckling.

TRUTH BE TOLD

It was early morning hours. Nia and I were wrapped up in my bed asleep.

"Get up, I need you to take me to the package you got a couple of months, an Amazon box. It had to be a medium-sized box. I need it," Big Mama woke me out of my sleep and demanded.

My mama had a key to my house. They both came into the room looking crazed.

"Mama, y'all, it's six a.m. in the morning. What are y'all doing here? An Amazon box? What the hell," I responded, looking puzzled. I had never cursed in front of my Big Mama before. I was still groggy and sleepy. I did not know if I was still dreaming or if they were really in my house at this time in the morning.

Big Mama said, "This is not a game. I need to see that box, Celeste, before anything else happens."

I got up quickly as soon as she said that. She looked worried. For her to ask me for something so random but specific meant something was gravely wrong.

I sat up in my bed, put on shoes, and went to my closet. I never did open that box. I had no idea what I had done with it. There was so much that happened after the box I didn't give it much thought. It was the same Amazon box that Ms. Jackson walked over to me.

"Big Mama, the lady across the street delivered that box to me. She said the Amazon driver had dropped it off on her porch by mistake," I explained.

"She had told me that the package had been delivered to her in error. Now that I think about it, that did not sit right with me."

"That's what I thought. That's the vision that I saw," she said.

"Are y'all gonna tell me what's going on, or are we just going to keep going in circles about an Amazon box?" I asked.

"Once we find the box, I will have better answers for you, Celeste. For now, please concentrate on where you put the box!" she yelled.

My mama was abnormally silent. I had never seen her this quiet before. I usually keep boxes and junk in my garage. I went into the garage and rummaged through anything that closely resembled a medium-sized brown box. I sorted through several boxes before I saw a box that had the black letters "Amazon" written on it.

There it was, sitting on top of a few plastic containers of hair products.

I found it.

I could hear my mama and Big Mama having somewhat of an argument. They thought I was still in the garage looking for the box.

"You should have told her months ago, years ago," I heard Big Mama say.

"Ma, I did not want to worry her for no reason. Up until Mia, it really wasn't a reason to even bring all of this old stuff up," my mama responded.

"You have exactly three minutes to think about how you are going to tell her or I'm gonna do it," Big Mama implored.

I walked into the entrance of the kitchen. Big Mama did not waste time opening the box. She had a box cutter in her hand. She moved like a ninja. The box seemed like an ordinary box to me.

Finally, after all the cutting, she got the box open. It was just a normal ugly shirt enclosed in plastic that I did not order. I would not be caught dead in that shirt, but it wasn't the time for fashion notables. In the shirt were carefully placed small bones, there small, little bones that were hard to detect.

"That's what I was looking for right there," Big Mama said.

She carefully placed all the contents back in the Amazon box and asked me and Mama to come join her in the living room. She removed all the bones and put them in a napkin.

"Unfortunately, Celeste, someone had very ominous plans for you. They wanted you to suffer badly. In other words, someone used dark roots to exact some type of revenge," she said angrily.

"But I didn't bother or hurt anyone. I barely speak to anyone other than my friends. It couldn't be one of them. Who would want to harm me? Why? I really don't have ill will towards anyone," I professed.

I thought for a minute. That fucking Snow or Lawrence did some dark magic shit, causing my life to crumble to nothing. Maybe it was Ms. Gladys, but she hates everybody. Mrs. Jackson practiced roots, or at least that's what the neighbor reported. Maybe it was her. She was the one that brought the box over in the first place. But why? Why would she do something so cruel. It caused my baby to die. It caused my child's death.

Mama finally got her words together to speak.

"Celeste, I really think this is all my fault. It's so much I should have told you. I just did not want to bring unnecessary drama into your world. I know Mrs. Jackson better than you think. We did go to high school together. But there was more," Mama confessed.

"Mama, what does any of this have to do with the package, dark roots, or Mrs. Jackson?" I asked.

"Let me finish, I'm getting to that part. Mrs. Jackson had a husband, Richard. I also had a relationship with Richard that resulted in a pregnancy, you," she continued.

"Wait, my daddy is not my daddy? He's Richard, Mrs. Jackson's dead husband?" I asked, shocked.

"Yes, that is correct. Richard is your biological father, but I never told him who you were or anything about you. Evelyn is Mrs. Jackson's first name. She was with Richard for a few years right after high school. He and I messed around periodically until I got pregnant and left. I left to be with your dad, Malachi. Evelyn hated me getting pregnant from Richard. I allowed them all to think that I was pregnant from Malachi, your dad. Somehow Evelyn found out that you were indeed Richard's daughter, probably the dark magic. I firmly believe as soon as she found this information out, she started plotting something horrible to make me pay for having his baby," my mom said.

I was in shock. I found out that my dad was not my real dad. This was that bullshit off Lifetime Movie Network. All this time, she had known Mrs. Evelyn Jackson better than she had let on. This was a fucked-up secret. Had I known, I would not have stayed six months across the street from someone who hated my existence.

Big Mama chimed in, "We have a bigger beast to deal with other than the identity of your real dad. I saw in a dream that Evelyn handed you a box. That's why I came over here in a panic. The ritual we did at the my house while you were asleep revealed that someone close in proximity was trying to harm you," Big Mama said.

I had no words. My father, dark roots, and the death of my baby seemed overwhelming. I understood, but I could not process everything that was going on. I had just really started to accept that Mia was gone. Then I found out that Mrs. Jackson was trying to harm me on purpose. She had actually been successful at fucking up my job and having my baby killed. What a bitter fucking bitch! Now I wanted revenge. I wanted to go over to her house, snatch her out of bed, and beat that bitch lifeless. Even if her husband cheated on her and got a baby, she had no right to bring that type of harm to my family.

Big Mama found it to be a personal insult that an Evelyn Jackson went after her own blood and she did not see it coming. That was mostly because I kept her out of my business. She was well intent on avenging Mia's death. There was no need to deal with the shooter; he killed himself at the scene. There was no mystery to solve there. However, Big Mama made it crystal clear that she had to avenge Mia, me, and her reputation. I thought back to that night I was at her house. Big Mama, my mama, and those ladies had conjured up something, but I had no idea what it was at the time. I was in the midst of forces that I did not understand.

"Now that we are all caught up, Celeste, go get my bag out of the living room. Denise, you clear the table," Big Mama ordered.

She cut off all lights in the house. Mama made sure the door was shut so that Nia would not wake up. She lit three candles and put a dark cape of drape of some sort. We all stood around the table, watching her work. She chanted something in another language that I could not understand. She asked me to write the name Evelyn Jackson on a piece of paper. She took the paper from my hands and folded it in threes. Big Mama tore the paper in three sections. The first section she burned over the black candle itself. The second piece she put in cup of water sitting on the table. The last piece was interesting. She took it outside along with a candle and the bones from the shirt. She went across the street in Mrs. Jackson's yard and burned the last piece paper. She let all the ashes fly over Evelyn Jackson's yard. She then took those bones out of her pocket and sprinkled them in her yard.

Big Mama was fearless.

We watched from the window as Big Mama walked back across the street and into the house.

She sighed with a sense of relief, like the deed was complete.

"Ladies, I will be staying here, right here with Celeste for the next couple of days just to make sure everything goes through," she said without asking.

I did not know what she meant by "everything goes through." But I felt comforted that she was with me to fight a battle that I could not see.

"Big Mama, what's going to happen next if she put some type of roots on me?" I asked.

She sat down comfortably in the chair.

"You gone be *al right*. Don't worry our pretty little head about that damn Evelyn Jackson no mo," she said.

Mama asked her, "Do you think that all this is over? I mean, are Celeste and Nia protected?" she questioned.

"Well, baby, I don't usually practice dark spells, but in this case, I had no choice. She will pay for all of the harm that she caused you and this family. And, she won't be harming anyone else," she said reassuringly.

I had so many questions about this story. The guilt was eating my mama up from the inside, I could tell.

"I don't blame you, Mama, for any of this," I said.

Mrs. Jackson was a bitter, evil lady who was mad about an outside child and decided to make my life as miserable as possible. She was also a damn murderer. She killed the nurse down the street and my real dad. She had my daughter killed and who knows what else she had planned in her malicious head.

I'm still gonna fuck her old ass up when I see her, I said to myself.

STREET JUSTICE

I had taken all the time I could. It was time to return to work. I had no feelings; my life was numb. I had gone outside to get some fresh air. My mama had stayed with me just to make sure I was okay to go to work. She had planned to drive me. Of course, Nia wasn't going to the school ever again. They had not opened her school up anyway after the shooting.

I stared across the street because I wanted to knock the shit out of Mrs. Jackson. She had caused so much turmoil in my life she needed to pay for it. I know Big Mama did her thing, but I wanted to do mine.

I stayed out there for a while and did not see her come out. My phone rang. It was Kade.

"Celeste, I have been trying to reach you. I came by your house, your job and called you every single day. I'm sorry, baby. You know that I loved those girls like they are my own. Mia, I feel sick about it. I have their bicycles in my truck and would at least like to bring Nia her bicycle, if that is okay with you," he said.

I was actually happy to hear from Kade. He was very close to the girls. I do remember seeing him at her funeral, but I was in no shape to talk.

"Yes, you can bring the bicycle by later if you like, just bring the one bike. Give the other one to Goodwill or something," I responded.

"I would love to see you both. Talk to you after work," he stated before hanging up.

I walked back in the house to grab my work bag. My mama got Nia ready and got her in the car. Just as she finished fastening Nia's seat belt, she looked up and saw Evelyn Jackson emerge from her house and walk to her mailbox.

Denise Belle (my mama) caught a glimpse of her and trotted over to meet her at the mailbox.

Mrs. Jackson looked distressed to see Mama heading toward her. She tried to retreat, but Mama got there faster than either one of us anticipated.

I returned to the car and saw what was happening. Mama had caught up with her and confronted her.

"You jealous, dreadful bitch, did you really think you would get away with this shit?" my mama said before she swung and hit her in the face.

Mrs. Jackson went down like a broken tree limb. Mama got on top of her and slapped both sides of her face. Evelyn Jackson tried to scream, but every time she opened her mouth, Denise threw another punch to the face, silencing her.

I ran over to get my mama off her before someone called the police. After about five punches and four kicks to the abdomen later, Mama finally got up and allowed me to assist her back to the car. As I pulled my mama off her, I sneaked in a side kick to the face.

"I'm gonna call the police on you home-wrecking bitches. No, I got something else for both of you whores," she said, picking herself off the ground slowly.

Her nose was bloody, and her shirt was torn. I noticed that her lips were swollen and dripping blood.

I was going to fight that old bitch, but Denise Belle beat me to it. What a great way to start the day! I was surprised that Big Mama didn't hear the commotion of the fight. That was probably best. I was thinking on the whole tribulation. The only rationale I could think of was, Mrs. Jackson did not bother Mama directly because Big Mama had some type of protective cloak over her. They should have had one over me and the girls. What the hell were they thinking?

We sat in the car for a moment in disbelief that my mama had just whooped Evelyn's ass, old-fashioned style.

Mrs. Jackson had gone back in the house to clean herself up. She was a mess. She also had threatened us again!

We drove off and looked at each other. For about three minutes, we didn't say a word. I burst out laughing suddenly.

"Mama, you just had a real fight in the neighbor's yard. I can't believe what I just saw," I ranted.

I was the driver, and Mama was in the passenger's seat. She looked to the back seat and apologized to Nia.

"I'm sorry you had to see your Mimi act like that, pumpkin, but sometimes fighting is the answer," she said to her.

I waited outside to fight her, then I got distracted by my phone call. Lord, help me and my crazy life. Mama was just as angry as I was, if not more. The guilt she felt as a parent had to be tremendous. In addition, she and I both knew that I still had to deal with work and Keith.

"Celeste, she had that shit coming. I don't even want to hear your mouth," she scolded.

I agreed with her. Evelyn Jackson had that shit coming and some more. I never believed in roots. I thought that for it to work, all parties had to believe in it. That heartless bitch conjured up some dark spirit to take my precious angel from me and wreak havoc in my life. Unfortunately, it worked.

That ass whooping was just the beginning for her. Big Mama assured me of that.

I had to get my mind right. It was my first day back to work since the shooting. Mama was keeping Nia for the day. I hoped she had cooled down.

As we pulled up to the school, I saw a full parking lot. I did not feel like the questions, stares, or hugs from people who really didn't like me. Mama told Coia and Nikki to meet us in the parking lot so that I would have support going into the building.

They were standing there, waving at me like I was a kid in their class.

"Mama, thank you... Words can't... I could not get it out," I said to her. I almost started to cry.

"You got to be strong, Celeste. Nia is good, I'm good, and you are good, okay?" she said. She was about to cry the more she looked at my face.

Crazy Coia came over to greet Mama. She reached all the way in the car and gave Nia a bear hug.

"Hey, pretty girl, how are you?" Coia asked her.

Nia hugged her back. "Hey, TT, I'm not going to school today." Coia talked with her a few more minutes until we reached the moment of truth.

Mama drove off. As Coia, Nikki, and I walked up to the building, they decided to fill me in on all the gossip.

"Girl, these bitches ain't changed a bit in this last month. Snow is still a wretched ho, the old school twins think they running shit, and Lawrence don't even look in my face. They know I'm a time bomb ready for action," Coia bragged. "For one month, I have been waiting on one of them to slip and say something fucked up about you or what happened. Happy to report they have been on their best behavior."

Nikki started in on her conversation.

"I worked with your sub to make sure the kids had work and were behaving. They missed you so much. They asked how you were doing every single day. I did not have to explain what was going on because it was all over the news for the past three weeks," she elaborated.

We had reached the door. And I could see a line of teachers in the hall gazing at me as if they had seen a celebrity. Coia walked in first like a protective shield. I walked in the middle, and Nikki sandwiched me in. They wanted to make sure that I was not ambushed by stupid questions and dumb-ass statements.

Keith met me at the door. He practically had to ask Coia for permission to speak to me.

"I just want to get Ms. Belle the proper welcome she deserves," he said.

Keith motioned me over to the side. "I'm sorry for your loss. But, nothing has changed. You're still surplused. Make sure that you start cleaning your classroom out, please, and thank you."

He pulled me to the side to tell me that shit. I had just lost my child, and he wanted to be an asshole. He would pay for that shit.

I thought that was real fucked up. We didn't talk about anything that happened previously. He then tried to give me a fake-ass pat on the back like he was being supportive. Everyone was watching, especially his simple-ass girlfriend.

She watched us closely. I hate the both of them. There was an outpour of "We are so sorry... We are here for you... We support you" from most of the teachers and staff.

I walked into the teachers' lounge to get my mail. Mrs. Snow happened to be in there at the time. She looked me up and down, scanning my face for signs of sadness or disparity. She rolled her eyes and walked past me.

I looked slightly different. I had lost about 20 lb. with all the stress of losing Mia. My clothes fit me more loosely than before. I was still pretty, my hair was still done, and I still dressed to impress. But sorrow had shown its ugly face in mine. I could not hide that.

Snow did not say anything to me. She was just petty! My security guards were standing right outside the door, Coia and Nikki.

She walked back out without saying anything to me. I'm so glad 'cause I would have been on that ass like Mama was on Mrs. Jackson this morning.

Nikki walked with me upstairs to class. She taught next door, so that was convenient. When I walked in my classroom, I saw that my students created for me a huge banner that read, "We love you, Ms. Belle." It made me teary! I missed my babies so much. My students make the job worthwhile. My first-period class came in unaware that I was back. Once they all were seated, I came in from the closet and surprised them. They all jumped up at the same time and ran over to hug me. I had not felt that good since before Mia died.

They buzzed around me for the first thirty minutes of class. Needless to say, they didn't get any work today. One of my kids wanted to know if Nia was okay. I talked about the girls so much in class the students knew them. I thought that was sweet. I was still not at a point where I could talk about it publically.

Around fourth period, I saw that I had 147 emails that needed to be cleared. I deleted a lot. Then I saw an email from Meredith Reyes. I had almost forgotten about her. She was such a kind soul.

I know things are really tough for you right now.
Please know you have a friend in me whenever you
need me.

—Meredith

She was going to give me a verbal recommendation to a new school. I saved her email so that I could contact her later.

I sifted through other emails; some were of various trainings coming up. Others were end-of-the-year procedures and processes.

I was surprised to see an email from Dereck. He had taken a job in our district. The day he told me, that was the same day my life changed forever. I could not even be happy for him because of my personal concerns. Dereck had taken a promotion in our district and apparently was assigned to twenty schools. Our school was included in the twenty. According to the email, he would be out next week to a school and meet the school staff. One email caught me off guard. Keith had submitted my name for the assistant principal's program months ago when we were in a good place. They finally responded; I was in the pool for being in the final selection.

I had forgotten all about that. It was the single most decent thing he had done for me, ever. He must have forgotten, or he would have taken that nomination back also!

Coia drove me home. I was relieved that the first day back went relatively easy. I was exhausted. I just wanted to go to sleep. Coia dropped me off at my house. Part of me expected the police to be waiting at the door to arrest my mama. She beat the shit out of Mrs. Jackson. I described the whole daddy thing and the fight from this morning. For once in life, Coia was speechless. She was more shocked than she was angry.

"I don't usually believe in roots and voodoo and shit, but this makes perfect sense. I remember your Big Mama used to read people's palms all of the time," Coia indicated.

I had forgotten all about the palm readings she used to do.

"Why didn't you tell me that old bitch was giving you a hard time? I would have done some shit like glued her lips shut, put hot sauce in her eye solution, or fuck up all of her good wigs."

We both started laughing. It felt good to laugh again. I felt partially guilty for being able to laugh while my baby was deceased.

Kade came over about 6:00 p.m. I was standing in the driveway when Kade pulled up. He was wearing Levi's jeans that fit like a glove. Kade was a fine specimen of a man. He had slimmed down quite a bit. He had a stomach that I was attracted to. His University of Miami jersey snuggled his torso with an exact fit. He reached into his truck and pulled out a little Disney Princess bicycle for Nia. He rolled the bicycle beside my leg. Once he was in arm's length, Kade grabbed me by my waist and hugged me like we were long-lost lovers. I didn't care if he was seeing someone. I kissed his lips like we had just started dating.

We walked inside and spoke to my mom. She was happy to see him. Mama loved Kade. He treated me and the girls very well. She always compared him to Promise, only to highlight all the qualities that Promise didn't have. Mama always called Kade her son-in-law. I never told her I suspected that he was dating his coworker. Her plan was always for us to be together. She told me how stupid I was for messing things up with him.

Kade had not been to my house since Mia died. When he brought the bicycle in for Nia, he still looked around for Mia as if she was going to pop out from around the corner. He grabbed my hand for support. He was hurt being in the house and not seeing both of the twins. He played with Nia for a little while.

"Are you ladies hungry? I can go pick something up if you like," he announced to Big Mama and my mama. He was such a gentleman.

"Not this time, son-in-law, but I insist upon a rain check," Mama said to Kade.

I thanked him for coming over and walked him out.

"Hey, the next time I text you, answer me, man," he requested.

UNLEASHED

Dereck arrived to Pine River Middle with an entourage. There were at least twelve of them in total. They all met in the conference room to discuss his new position.

Mr. Lawrence, Mr. Smith, and the team leaders all met with Dereck's team. I saw Ms. Snow head into the meeting looking a tacky mess. Her eyes met mine. She turned her nose up in my direction and headed to join the group in the conference room. She was leaving the restroom. When she switched directions and headed for the conference room, I noticed that her long skirt was tucked in the top of her panties. It was flipped up, exposing her granny panties. She was about to enter her most important meeting this year with her dress tucked in the top of her underwear. She was a scrawny little thing. I laughed my ass off. If she was a friend, I would have stopped her from embarrassing herself. But she wasn't a friend!

Snow sauntered away in her manly golf shoes, velvet shirt, and panties exposed. That made my day.

I went upstairs to my class to create lesson plans for the next few weeks of school. Third period was almost over.

During my planning period, I decided to go make sure that all my paperwork was in order for taking extended leave. That meant I have to see Ms. Gladys. I did not dread it this time. She was one of few staff who called to check on me while I was bereaving.

As I went downstairs, I ran into the old school twins. The big mean bully whispered something to the other while I walked down the hall. I could not hear her, but it was something snide. I was not in the mood for any bullshit.

She became quite bold.

"I'm serious, when you do ugly things, God will punish you and sometimes your kids," she bragged. She was talking to the other hag.

She said it loud enough for me to hear her. In her twisted way, she basically said Mia deserved to die. The other stooge just nodded in agreement. There was no compassion, nor did it compute. I was mentally frail and not in a good headspace for that comment.

We were in the center of the hall between two classrooms. I walked up to her and asked her, "What did you say?"

"You heard me. I said God don't like ugly," she repeated. I mustered up the strength of Hercules without any regard to the job.

I took one step closer to her. Without either one of us expecting it, I reached up and slapped the shit out of her. I tried to leave my handprint in her face. I slapped her wig crooked. She screamed, "Bitch, are you crazy?" Respusia grabbed her face.

Her friend said, "I'm telling Mr. Lawrence right now. You are out of control."

The moment that she said the word "control," Mr. Smith, the assistant principal, emerged from one of the side classrooms. He was so quiet that we had no idea he was there. He looked at me and addressed me first.

"Are you okay, Ms. Belle?" he asked.

I responded, "Yes, sir." The comment got the better of me, and a tear rolled down my cheek.

He then turned his attention to "Respusia."

"Mrs. Taylor, you had absolutely no business referring to or talking about the death of her seven-year-old child. You should know better. If I was her, I would have slapped you too. Say one word, and I promise you will be packing up and moving to another school by close of business tomorrow," he concluded.

The other teacher remained silent.

"This is the last time I'm going to have this conversation, am I clear?" Mr. Smith directed at them both.

That didn't go the way I thought that it would. I was pleasantly surprised.

"Ms. Belle, step in here for a minute, please," he requested.

He brought me into a nearby classroom and wanted to talk.

"Ms. Belle, those ladies were wrong for making a joke out of your tragic loss. I heard everything, even some parts you didn't hear. But you can't go around slapping the shit out of people," he continued.

I paused for a moment with a tear still falling on my cheek. We both laughed at the comment. He actually said "shit."

"Baby girl, I strongly suggest you get some counseling. You need it with everything that you have been through. I'm talking to you like I would my own daughter. You need a way to deal with all of your emotions. If you need me, I'm here. Don't hesitate to ask me for help. One more thing, you're a smart young lady Stop wasting your time with people who don't appreciate you," he advised.

I am grateful that he stopped me when he did. I was about to DDT the other old school twin.

I knew what Mr. Smith meant by his comment. Keith just used me for sex then looked for an excuse to kick me to the curb for the next flavor of the month.

I did deserve better. Mr. Smith stood up and handed me a card from his pocket. It was the number to a psychiatrist. I knew he was right. I needed to talk to a professional. I can't continue pushing people downstairs and slapping people. I gave him a daughterly hug and told him, "Thank you so much." It was an emotional thank-you.

I finally made it downstairs to the main office. Mrs. Gladys was sitting at her desk, filing papers in an accordion folder. She saw me walk through the door. She got up from her desk and hugged me. I was scared because she didn't hug people.

"Ms. Belle, I have all of your documents ready," she said. She softened up in the past four weeks.

"The leave forms have been backdated to make it easier on you," she added. I was partially in shock, but I know death changes people, not just the direct victim.

"Your surplus agreement is also in here. But don't sign it yet," she implied.

She winked her eye at me like she knew important information that I didn't know.

I took the paper folder and thanked her. Wow, she was a totally different person. It felt good to have so much support from my coworkers.

Nothing changed in the time that I was gone. We had another after school meeting today. I did not miss this bullshit at all. Coia and Nikki saved me a seat.

"Hey, Celeste, I heard this meeting is supposed to be juicy," Nikki said.

"OOOH, do tell," Coia responded.

We all settled in quickly. There were several dignitaries at the meeting. We had to be on our best behavior. It's so sad because adults are worse than the students in faculty meetings, talking, laughing, playing on their phones, etc.

Dereck Archer, the new deputy superintendent, introduced himself to the faculty. I could hear the low remarks and comments made about how fine he was.

"Good afternoon, everyone. This is a fine group of people sitting before me. I wanted to introduce myself and my team as we will be visiting quite often," Dereck explained.

"As you know, the only thing constant in education is 'change.' With that being said, Mr. Lawrence will be moving on to another school. He's done great work here, and now his services are needed at an elementary school effective June 30," he disclosed.

We all looked at each other amazed. None of us saw it coming. Coia said to me, "Yes, my prayers have been answered," as she explained it. He was focused on pussy, not the job. The kids don't need that shit. And you definitely don't need that messy shit in your life. She was correct even if I did not want to admit it.

A few minutes of shock and chatter surrounded the room.

"I have one more announcement. Your very own Mr. Smith will be promoted to the position of principal," Dereck said.

We all stood up and clapped, excited for his promotion. The room was full of cheers and high fives for Mr. Smith. Mr. Lawrence's movement seemed more like a demotion. No one really acknowledged it. That was strange; in Vegas, they seemed like best buddies.

The three of us decided to reserve the rest of our comments until we got to the parking lot. That's where the most sacred conversations were held. Mr. Smith was encouraged to say a few words.

He led with, "I am delighted to be the new leader at Pine River with the best group of teachers in South Florida. This has always been my home, and you guys are family. Also, please check the surplus list. Some changes have been made."

Keith did not stay around for talking. He retreated to his office. Mr. Smith stayed around to answer questions.

Coia and Nikki went to look at the surplus list. I did not bother. I was already surplused. If anything, they would just add to the list, not eliminate names. Snow was looking crazy as hell. I'm sure Keith told her about the changes well in advance.

Coia was the first to get to the list. "Back up, give a sister some space to read," she barked at other teachers trying to see the new list.

The old school hags had been here for over a decade. There was no reason for them to check the list.

Coia reviewed the list and ran back to the table. "Outside right now, right now," she insisted.

We tried to look as professional as possible while sprinting out of the room.

"Number A, bitch, you not on the list no mo'," Coia informed me.

"Number B, the old school twins are out of this mutherfucker, you hear me? GONE," she said excitedly.

That was a relief. I did not know how to react to the news. I thought for sure I was gone! I could still teach with my besties! While the old school hags laugh at my daughter's death, I hope they think their reassignment is funny too. You got slapped and lost your teaching position all in one day bitch! But we were still stuck with Snow's lame ass.

It was a great day overall. Mr. Smith had my back, Mrs. Gladys gave me a heads-up, and I was able to keep my job.

I pulled in front of the mailbox to get my mail. I noticed Evelyn's car was not in the driveway. That bitch got her ass whooped.

She probably didn't want part two and went to stay with family or somebody.

As I sorted through the mail, I saw something for "the parent of Mialondra Thomas." It was a check. The check was written for 250,000 dollars. It was an insurance check. I had forgotten all about the life insurance that I had on each of the girls. Somehow in all the madness, I submitted her death certificate to the insurance company, or maybe Mama did it for me.

SERVED COLD

The weekend had finally arrived. It had been a couple of days since the front-yard fight. I looked across the street and saw an unfamiliar car. A strange lady was leaving Mrs. Jackson's house. I had never seen her before. Mrs. Jackson's car was not in the yard. The lady came back out with boxes and other packages. Another car pulled up. This time, it was a couple of guys. None of them looked familiar. Usually, if Mrs. Jackson saw me outside, she would find some excuse to torment me. Those wrestling moves Mama put on her ass stopped that real quick. I was cleaning out my trunk. When Keith told me I was still being surplused, I started packing up classroom items.

Keith was a real asshole for that bullshit. On my first day back, he wanted to make me feel real small. I should have asked Big Mama to put some roots on his evil ass. But fate worked things out for me. Now his ass has to pack!

Curiosity was eating at my soul. I was curious if she took a mini vacation or something.

I walked over to the yard. "Excuse me, I am Mrs. Jackson's neighbor. Is she alright? I have not seen her in a few days," I investigated.

A middle-aged man with a potbelly and an afro came over to me. "Nice to meet you. I'm her nephew. Aunt Evelyn was in a car wreck on I95 two days ago. She was traveling north when a truck lost control, jackknifed, and ran right into her. Her vehicle was struck so hard that it split in half. The force of the truck decapitated her. We are here trying to get some of her things in order. As you know, she had no kids," he detailed.

"I'm sorry for your loss," I said, but I wasn't.

I went back home in shock. What did Big Mama do? She did that ritual three days ago. I thought I would feel relieved that she was dead, but everything had turned so dark and morbid. It was just hard to see simplicity. I raced in the house where Big Mama was packing her suitcase.

"Big Mama, where are you going?" I asked, disappointed.

"Celeste, I told you when my work was done, I was going back home. I need to water my garden and treat my pond, you know, grandma kind of stuff," she said.

She knew what happened before I did. Her work was done. She came for revenge, and she got it. I wondered if roots could break a leg, cut off a finger, or something less severe than death.

I was going to miss Big Mama. She made me feel safe and cooked the best meals.

"I...we...are going to miss you *so* much," I said in complete sobs. The crying said so much more than what words could say.

"I know, I know, don't cry. You are welcome, sweet pea. You just bring Nia to visit her Big Mama soon. We have gotten close," she instructed.

"Of course, I will. I love you so much. Please don't get mad at me if I call you every day," I teased.

She had been trying to get me to call for months before things turned fatal, but I did not listen. That will never happen again. She kissed me on the cheek and waited for Mama to get there. Nia played with her until Mama arrived.

I could not wait until Mama got in the door. I wanted to tell her every sullen detail. Mrs. Jackson was dead, I mean decapitated dead!

"Mama, you won't believe...," I said before she stopped me. She put her finger up toward my face. It stopped the words from coming out of my mouth instantly.

"The work is done, we will never discuss it," she said. I did not know the rules of voodoo or dark rituals. But "the work is done" was code for revenge exacted.

I let that marinate for a while. Part of me was happy that we got justice for Mia, but another part of me knew that something in the mix was wrong. The deed was done, and I could not take it back.

They got on the road about six to travel back to the country. I prayed nothing happened to them like what happened to Mrs. Jackson. I was a little skittish about death with all I had seen. As I was washing clothes, Dereck sent me a text.

> D: You busy tonight?
> M: I have Nia tonight, no sitter.
> D: That's too bad. I wanted to taste you.
> M: Rain check, please.

I thought Dereck was awesome. But I was not about to get into another Keith situation. I really wanted to try to work things out with Kade. I had done so much damage to our relationship. It was going to take drastic measures to win his attention over, especially since he was involved.

I called Kade and invited him to lunch. I had to use my sympathy card. It was all that I had.

I texted him a message.

> C: Having a rough day. Could use a shoulder to cry on. Meet me for lunch tomorrow.
> K: Of Course, friend. I have two if you need them.
> C: Great! Meet me at my house tomorrow about noon.

I started planning the day. "Nia, you want to go to the store with Mommy?" I yelled.

"No, Mommy, my daddy coming to pick me up soon, remember?" she reminded me. I had forgotten Promise was really stepping things up with Nia. I guess with the loss of Mia, he figured time was not promised to anyone.

I waited a couple of hours. Promise pulled up in the driveway. He came alone this time.

"Hey, Big Head," he said to me. This was his playful tone. Since Mia, we both made great efforts to get along better.

"Hey, Big Ears," I said back. We hugged.

"What you and Nia up to this weekend?" I asked.

He usually would tell me none of my damn business, but today was different. We were different.

"I'm taking my baby to get a pretty dress. Then, I'm taking her to dinner and a movie. She should be good and tired when we get home if you want to come over," he said as he nudged me on the shoulder. We were in such a wonderful place. I did not want to ruin it with sex, not even good sex.

"I'll think about it," I responded. In reality, I wasn't going anywhere! I was holding out for Kade.

The store was crowded, but I managed to get everything that I needed. The menu consisted of his favorites: wine, strawberries, seafood salad, Ritz crackers, and wings from Hip Hop. I spent the evening cooking the seafood salad. The rest was ready-made.

It was April and sundress season. The humidity in Miami was almost unbearable. I made sure to wear a dress that was airy with thin material since it was so hot. The entire back of the dress was out, but the remainder of the dress was form fitting.

Kade got there at twelve o'clock on the dot. He came to the door like a true gentleman and brought me flowers.

It was so adorable. I asked him to get the wine out of the freezer and grab the picnic basket on the table. Kade seemed surprised that I had put so much effort into a simple Sunday lunch.

"Damn, Celeste, you went all out for ya boy. Do I smell Hip Hop wings?" he asked excitedly.

"Yes, you do, and a few other surprises in there also," I added.

Kade drove his car and asked, "Where to?" We headed to Brickell Park. I wanted a nice waterfront view. It was gorgeous. He found us a perfect spot near the jogging trail facing the ocean. I laid a thick blanket down. Kade took his time going through the picnic basket like it was Christmas. For a while, it felt like old times, or better. He put his hand on my bare back. It was his version of comforting me.

"Seriously, how have you been doing with everything?" he asked. I did not want to scare him away with doom and gloom suicidal thoughts. I gave him a basic answer.

"Well, about as good as you can expect. This is still very new. I'm dealing with it the best I can. Nia is the real MVP. She just keeps on rolling with the punches. I'm learning from her. Oh, also, I go to counseling Monday," I explained.

We chatted back and forth between glasses of wine and small saucers of food. It was so romantic. I lay in his lap and laughed at all his corny jokes. Then we got to the serious part.

"So, what does your girlfriend think of you having brunch with an old friend?" I had to ask.

"Man, don't ruin a great date with that mess. But if you must know, we are not a couple. We just hook up from time to time," he informed me.

I was cool with that. I just needed to know if I still had a chance to be with him.

We ended the evening with a beautiful kiss.

"I love you too, baby," Kade said as he dropped me off. I smiled. My heart smiled.

My brother, Jerald called me shortly after getting in from my perfect date. He never calls me unless he wants something. What now, Jesus?

"Sis, check this shit out, I saw your boy. What's your principal's name, Keith or Kenny or some shit? Anyway, I just saw the nigga over by Liberty City. I walked up to the nigga and asked him if he knew Celeste Belle. First he told me I looked familiar. That's when he fucked up. I could not believe he said, 'I used to fuck with that ho, but ain't nothing special about her,'" he said, mad as fuck.

I was taken back that Keith was in Liberty City at all. Apparently, he did not recognize my brother from his brief school visit. Did Jerald say he called me a ho?

"Man...that ain't it though. Me and my boys was like, 'What that mutherfucka just said?' He kept saying crazy shit about my sister, man. I dropped that nigga with one hit, right in the parking. You they sister too, so they started kicking the nigga 'til an Arab who owned the store came out and stopped us. It was almost curtains for his ass, we wasn't fuckin off," Jerald said. He continued on his tirade.

What kind of principal talks about his employee that way? Jerald could have been a parent of a student, anyone. Why would he say such awful things about me? I didn't do anything that bad to him to deserve this treatment.

Shit, whatever the reason, he thought I called his wife, I said his dick was little, or I was sneaking behind his back in Vegas. He was married! He had no right to be mad! I thought my hate for him had dissolved, but I was wrong.

I'm glad Jerald beat his ass. This family was giving out ass whoopings like Floyd Mayweather. The lesson of the day was, don't let this teacher shit fool you. My people will fuck you up if you come for me!

SNOWSTORM

The bank didn't open until 9:00 am. I had to deposit this insurance check before I misplaced it. I was bad about losing checks and paperwork, the worst. I placed the check inside my wallet then put the wallet back inside my purse. I had never deposited this much money in a bank before. I wasn't sure how this would go. It was raining outside. The kids were supposed to have some type of field day. The rain would mess that up. I walked into the Credit Union at exactly 9:03 a.m. I signed up to speak with a bank representative. I handed the lady the check after I endorsed it. I explained that my daughter died. She stopped looking at her computer and gave me a heartfelt look. I had said those words so much that I was numb.

"I'm so sorry that happened to you," the lady said. "Oh my god, your baby was one of the kids shot at that private school," she stated. I nodded my head yes. She processed my check quickly, came around the desk, and gave me a hug. I appreciated her gesture, but I was still working through it all. I told her "thank you" and continued with the transaction. "There will be a thirty-day hold on the check due to the amount and nature of the check. I will talk to the manager about processing it much faster for you, honey," she explained. It was thoughtful of her to give me that type of attention.

My appointment with the psychiatrist was scheduled for 10:15 a.m. I got there with time to spare. I wasn't crazy. I wasn't going to kill... Well, that wasn't true. I had people to talk to. It was unnatural to share intimate details about your life with a complete stranger. After going through the certification process, I realized psychologists and psychiatrists are no more qualified to tell other people about their lives than a bartender. Their lives are just as fucked up as everyone else's.

"Good morning, Mrs. Belle. I am Dr. Allen. We will be scheduling you for biweekly sessions to discuss anything that you like or feel helpful," she said.

She started out with very general questions then went into my family dynamics. She asked about parents, siblings, then my children.

"I had a set of seven-year-old twins, but one was murdered in a school shooting a month and a half ago, I told her." I did not break down or fall apart. I just stared at the floor.

"That was very recent, Ms. Belle. How has this impacted your parenting with your other twin? Do you feel pretty good about returning to work so soon?" she asked. I told her I was fine to go back to work and stared at the floor some more.

"You know what, I would like to see you weekly just for the next few weeks. There is nothing wrong with you. The death of your daughter was so recent. It just would be a better idea than biweekly," she explained.

I did not argue. Things seemed fine, or better, but I know I was not 100 percent. I wasn't even 55 percent.

The rain had stopped from this morning. The sun had come out.

I arrived late to work, but it was a planned appointment. I had already discussed flex hours with Mr. Smith.

I wanted to see Keith.

The way Jerald explained it, he should be half dead. Or maybe he had the wrong person. I walked into the main office to let Mrs. Gladys know that I was in the building. I walked by Keith's office and saw that the door was closed. Maybe he was absent today.

I went upstairs to my class. The end of the year was approaching. The kids were doing makeup work. I was especially glad to see my school daughter, Destiny. So much had happened since Destiny revealed her awful family secret. I gave her a nonverbal thumbs-up. She flashed a smile back at me.

I had Nikki check on her while I was out. She coordinated with the social worker to follow up. Family services had been out to her home, and the stepdad was arrested. Her mother was so angry with Destiny for telling school officials that she ended up living with her maternal aunt. Destiny seemed fine with it. Kids are so resilient. Destiny had assigned herself to helping me this afternoon. If I could adopt that baby, I would.

It was an abbreviated day. The kids were having "outside" play. All teachers were assigned duties for the activities. The students were superexcited. When the bell rang for the festivities to start, I immediately went to my station. Destiny, my little helper, came with me.

Coia and I were serving snow cones. That was easy enough. We were in the best spot to see everything. Mr. Lawrence finally dragged his self in the office. He had on dark shades. Maybe he was wearing them because the sun was shining brightly outside. Or maybe he had them on 'cause my brother knocked the shit out of him. I needed to investigate further, from a distance of course. I really expected him to come up and curse me out or something, but he avoided me the entire day. Snow was following behind him like a lost puppy, taking him drinks and snacks and shit. I know other teachers noticed how desperate she looked.

It was hot as fish grease out on the football field. Coia had Destiny there to help her. I decided to go back into the office to cool down for a minute.

I sat down in the auditorium close to the office to cool off. I had dozed off, maybe from fatigue or just from being hot. I opened my eyes and realized I had missed dismissal. I could not believe that I had fallen asleep in the auditorium.

The buses had been called. Students had been dismissed. The hall was filled with tired, overheated teachers.

I saw a medium-sized Black lady wearing pajamas walk into the front door. It had to be a parent. She had two large luggage pieces in both of her hands. The lady would have been attractive had she bothered to put some makeup or comb her hair. The pajamas were just an atrocity. The lady was walking fast. Most of the teachers were congregated in the middle of the hall just in front of the entrance. I had a great view from the auditorium. I had no interest in going into the hallway.

I saw the lady stop in center of the hallway with luggage in tow. *Why the fuck would she bring luggage in a school?* I though. She had a wild look about her. The lady skimmed the hall quickly.

191

"Where is Mr. Keith Lawrence?" she asked. No one answered her. They all suspected she was an angry parent.

"Oh, let me be more clear, EXCUSE me. My name is Maranda Lawrence. My husband is Keith Lawrence. Do I have your attention now?" she asked.

I saw several teachers go in different directions to find Mr. Lawrence. Mr. Smith stepped up and asked her to follow him in the office and he would locate for Lawrence. She flat out refused.

"My husband is fucking someone here by the name of Tamara Snow, and I need to talk to her home-wrecking ass," she announced.

Every adult person in that hallway gasped in horror. The principal's wife was making a scene, and the person she accused was standing her coward ass right there. Every eye turned in the direction of Snow. She looked like she had seen a fucking ghost. Snow did not move from her spot or identify herself. Coia and Nikki looked at each other. They were about to point her ass out. I know it!

Keith came flying down the hall. He fought through the crowd of teachers with his shades still on his face. A blind man could see the embarrassment on his face. It was like watching a movie, live and in person. She walked up to him with the luggage dragging behind her. Thank God she did not say "Celeste Belle"!

"I'm sick of your shit. I brought your raggedy-ass luggage so you and your whore Tamara Snow can live happily ever after!" she screamed.

Keith grabbed a luggage piece from her and tried to shove her back out of the door. She did a football spin on his ass and dodged him. She opened the other luggage and started throwing his shit everywhere.

"Get his raggedy-ass draws with all the shit stains you can handle, his pants, but I cut the seat of 'em and take this toothbrush. He don't use it. He eats gum for fresh breath," she broadcast.

I laughed until I was in tears in the auditorium. No wonder his breath smelled like ass. He didn't brush his teeth. Oh god, this some *Love & Hip Hop* shit. *Baby*, all I needed was some popcorn.

"Maranda, how dare you come to my job acting like some crazy ghetto woman making this kind of scene," he said.

Keith tried to pick up as many items as he could off the floor.

He did everything he could to get her outside the doors. His wife wanted to send a clear message to Keith, Snow, and the rest of his groupies. Keith reached for her arm to yank her out the door. He resorted to physically removing her.

"Get your fucking hands off of me, I'm leaving. And I'm really leaving this time. When you get home, me and the girls will be gone!" she yelled. She stormed out of the door. He followed behind her. It was much easier to argue with his wife in the parking lot than to face his employees. This was an absolute nightmare for Keith and Snow.

The old school hags escorted Snow out of a side door to save her from a beatdown and shame. They thought we missed that part.

How could she ever show her face here again?

Coia and Nikki both looked around for me. They texted me at the same time.

C: BITCH, wya?
C: Auditorium, saw everything!

We all met up in the auditorium. "Let's take this shit outside," Coia said.

The teachers were all standing in the same place, discussing the events that had just unfolded. It was like someone had just pressed Pause on a movie.

Mr. Smith went back to his office shaking his head. He was a much wiser man than Keith. Mr. Smith valued his wife and valued his teachers. He would not compromise either.

Nikki ran upstairs and collected both of our purses. Coia met us near the cafeteria. We all exited through the bus loop. The front hall was a mess, sprinkled with nosy teachers and staff.

As we got to the parking lot, we could see Keith leaning against his truck, seething. He could have literally exploded. His head was in his hands without shades. We thought it wise to get in our cars and discuss this shit off campus.

One percent of me felt sorry for him. The other 99 percent thought he deserved every bit of this calamity.

Coia hosted the emergency gossip meeting. We grabbed some wings and went to her place. She lived fairly close to the school. It was very convenient.

"Okay, now who gonna start?" Coia asked.

"It's only right that I start things off since I barely dodged a bullet fucking around with Keith. *Girl*, I thought she was shooting his ass," I added.

"This crazy woman walked in the school with PJs on and luggage. What the fuck? Like did she plan this shit?" Nikki questioned.

I think we were all astonished that the principal's wife cut up like one of our parents. We all agreed that he had it coming. Going back to the conversation with Meredith, Keith had a pattern of cheating. Apparently, the wife got tired of that shit. It's embarrassing showing up at your husband's job, knowing he's cheating. Everyone looks at you crazy, laughing behind your back. They view the wife as the fool either for not knowing about the affair or for taking the cheating. It's a "no win" situation. While we all decompressed from a very exciting day, Kade called.

"Hey, Celeste, just checking on you and little Ms. Nia. How are you guys?" he asked.

I was really missing him. However, I did not want to be too forward and run him away again. I just responded that we were fine, considering.

"I was thinking we could go on another date, nothing special just to get reacquainted," he suggested.

I was thrilled that it was his idea. It's the best distraction to all the crazy at work and home.

"Of course, I'm down. What do you have in mind?" I inquired.

Kade carried on like it was some big secret. Either way, it would be great hanging out with him Saturday. He had a hectic schedule this week. At least the weekend we could unwind together.

CROSSROADS

There was a lot of activity across the street. A huge twenty-six-foot U-Haul truck was backed in Mrs. Jackson's driveway. I don't know why I was so interested in what was happening across the street. My enemy was gone! The family did not waste any time renting out Evelyn's house. A big lady came out of the house. She was large, as in five feet, eleven inches tall. The lady had long gray dreads with a large stomach. I needed a closer look just to see who would be moving next door. I went outside pretending to get something out of my trunk then the mailbox. The tall woman walked toward me. I sifted through the mail to look occupied.

"You must be Celeste," she said. I was shocked that she knew my name. I had never seen this woman before in my life.

"I'm Evelyn's sister, Aurelia, from Haiti," she said. The tall woman had wicked green eyes and scary hair that resembled tree branches growing in every direction of her head. She wore a black loose-fitting dress that draped over her huge frame. Aurelia did not extend her hand for introductions.

"My sister called me with some emergency to come visit her the night before she was killed. I will be living here until I finish some business," she said coldly.

I had no idea what to say after that. Aurelia's presence disturbed me. I don't know what Evelyn called and told her. Big Mama did something, but I'm not sure how much Evelyn knew. I felt very uncomfortable with this.

"Yes, ma'am. I'm her neighbor. I was her neighbor," I stammered. I walked away there without saying much.

The first thing I needed to do was call Big Mama. I said before, I don't know the rules to voodoo, dark curses, or revenge. For all I know, this lady was here to get revenge. She came right from the origin of voodoo, Haiti.

The phone rang three times before she picked up. "Big Ma, I don't want to alarm you, but Mrs. Jackson's sister, Aurelia, moved in her house from Haiti. She said something really weird about coming here for unfinished business, an emergency call from Evelyn," I rambled on.

I did not want to take the chance of anything happening to my Nia. She already took my other baby away from me. I don't know; maybe it would be Mama, Big Mama, or Kade. I could not take any loss.

"Calm down, me and your mama will check it all out. In the meantime, I want you to put your insurance money to good use and move out of that neighborhood," my Big Ma said calmly.

She was right. I needed to move. Evelyn and her sister had too much access to me and my family living next door.

I was late for my appointment but decided to give it another try. Same rule applied. I was never to speak of voodoo or family traditions of spells of any type.

Dr. Allen's office was empty. I would possibly make it to work by third period. She had a cup of coffee in her hand and seemed relaxed. I envied her for her ordinary, drama-less life.

"Good morning, Mrs. Belle. We are going to try a new approach today. I want you to write down the top five things that you want to work on or improve about yourself. No matter how big or small, write them in order of importance," Dr. Allen directed.

I was a teacher, not a psychologist. How the hell did I know where to start? There were so many things that needed work. Although it took me a while, I was able to concentrate on my weaknesses:

1. Promiscuity
2. Revenge
3. Parenting
4. Humility
5. Commitment

I handed her the list and sat back in the chair. Dr. Allen reviewed the list twice. I know they say "Don't judge," but of course they judge. If she really wanted to help, then this was it!

"Great, we have a starting point. Let's begin with promiscuity. What have you done to give you the impression that you are promiscuous?" she asked.

I wasn't sure how to respond to that. I just blurted something out. "Well, I like sex a lot. I have had sex with three partners during the same week. That seems excessive to me, but I enjoyed it," I responded.

She wrote down some notes and nodded.

"When was the last time you engaged in sex?" she asked.

I had to think about it. I had not had sex since Mia died. I just could not allow myself to feel that type of joy.

"Not since the death of my daughter," I confessed. She then indicated that perhaps my guilt of having sex the day that Mia was killed kept me from having sex. But that was not all; she then went deeper. She asked me if anything traumatic ever happened to me. I had an intact family. My daddy, brother, cousins, or uncles never tried to touch me inappropriately. Then the awful moment came back up. The time that I was raped in the alley behind the beauty shop.

"Do you want to tell me about that day?" Dr. Allen asked.

I responded by picking up my purse and walking out. I was not up for talking about that bullshit. The last memory I had of that day sent me to the hospital.

I abruptly ended the session and walked to my car. I just wanted to forget all about voodoo, rape, therapy, everything!

I should have taken the rest of the day off, but I decided to power through it. We had fifteen minutes left in second period. I decided to go in the teachers' lounge and have a cold drink. I knew that I was in a fucked-up place. I needed help sorting all my feelings and thoughts. I verbally promised myself not to get into any fights or physically attack anyone if I could help it.

Just as I made that pledge to myself, Snow walked into the teachers' lounge. After all the drama, no one expected Snow or Keith to be at work today. It was like she had a GPS on me.

FUCK! Why this bitch. I had just said I was in a bad headspace, but I was not gonna slap or push a bitch down the stairs today. God has such an interesting sense of humor. Snow came in the teachers' lounge and sat across from me. I knew that the Lord himself was testing me. Why would my archenemy sit down across from me?

Snow has never had two words to say to me. She had her head down, and her eyes looked watery as if she had been crying.

"I know you don't like me. Well, we don't like each other. I'm probably the last person that you would ever talk to. I don't understand why his wife came for me. She never came here and asked for you. Did you call her and tell her who I was?" she questioned.

I had to collect myself before I literally knocked her out of that damn chair she was sitting in.

"Why in the fuck would I call his wife? I don't care about you and Keith. I have a life, a man! Do you know how fucking stupid you look asking me this shit? You are investigating the wrong person. You probably should have stayed home and saved yourself the embarrassment. You gonna make me shoot your ass," I said.

I had no time to babysit her. How dare she ask me some shit like that? She paused before responding.

I didn't even give her time to react to my insults. I left the village idiot right there alone. I got my drink, bumped the damn table trying to get out of the door before I caught a charge.

I went by Coia's room to tell her about my encounter with Snow.

"Girl, she did not ask you that shit," Coia whispered. Her kids were taking a quiz. I could not interrupt her for long. I could not hold that information in.

"Yes, she did, and she wanted to know why the wife never came for me," I added. How stupid was that?

We had a brief laugh about it, then I returned to my class. The day started a little crazy. But by sixth period, it had leveled out. I was no longer angry or shocked. So much had happened to me. I was numb to much of life's recent mishaps.

During my ride, I decided that it was time to move forward with Kade. I loved him and wanted him. He understood why I had not been sexually active with him, but he deserved to be loved in every way!

The phone rang four times. Maybe it was a mistake. I dialed it again. Kade never ignored my calls. I was going to invite him to watch Disney movies with me and Nia. I thought it would be a great family moment for us.

Nia and I ate chocolate popcorn and nachos until we were stuffed. We were on the third Disney movie when Nia was out like a light. I was nodding between scenes. Since it was late, I laid Nia in bed then went to go shower.

My phone rang.

My recent trauma had me on high alert. I had my share of emergencies; 1:00 a.m. calls were never good. Coia called me.

"I wanted to tell you that Snow tried to commit suicide. She is in the hospital. I guess Keith broke up with her over the whole wife thing. She took several depressants and walked right in the middle of NE First Avenue. A car banged her up pretty bad," Coia said. "The only reason I know is 'cause Dre's sister is a nurse there and told me."

I felt horrible for her. She reached out to me today, and I treated her like shit. Snow did not deserve to go through this shit. Keith was leaving a trail of brokenhearted women.

"Is she alive, living?" I asked.

"I'm not sure how bad it is. I just wanted you to know."

Why did I hurt for a woman who treated me badly and mocked me for months? The tears rolled down my face. The guilt consumed me. I disliked her just because she was messing around with Keith. I felt more empathy for her than that sorry-ass Keith who put her in that position.

I stayed up for another two hours thinking of how I could have handled this situation better.

I was wide awake at 3:00 a.m.

The house was silent. This was the loudest silence I had ever heard. My thoughts were shouting in my head. It was too silent to sleep.

My doorbell rang. The doorbell rang again.

I turned on the porch light and saw that it was Kade. What the fuck was he doing here at this time in the morning? I opened the door.

He came in. Kade had been drinking, heavily.

"Kade, what are you doing here this time in the morning?" I asked.

"I needed to see you, I wanted to see my family," he responded.

"You did not seem that concerned about your family when I called you earlier," I responded.

I turned my back on him and sat down in a chair. He followed behind me. "Celeste, just come sit down on the couch with me. Let's talk, baby," he asked.

"Kade, I called you at six p.m. today, and you come by here unannounced nine hours later. What the fuck? I was really trying to make this shit work. But, I'm not going to be caught up in your love triangle. I know you were with your girlfriend from work," I said.

After the news about Snow, I was not in the mood for any man trying to run game on me.

"Yes, I was with her. But, I went to break things off. She wanted to get to keep things going. We argued, and I left. I did not answer your call because I had to sort through all of this shit. I broke up with her because I wanted to give our relationship a real try," he said.

How stupid did he think I was? I practically invented lies and excuses for not returning a call.

"Kade, don't play with me IN MY FACE. You were over there probably having breakup sex and it got late. I was an afterthought," I argued.

"No, baby, I promise you, when I broke up with her, I went to my frat brother's house and had a few drinks, more than a few drinks," he affirmed.

I decided that at three thirty in the morning, I was done arguing. I did not want to wake Nia. Kade was too fucked up to go home. I couldn't have that on my conscience if something happened to him.

He passed out on the couch. I went to get him a comforter and covered his drunk ass up.

I did not buy his story at all. Breakups are never clean-cut like that. There are tears, pleading, bargaining, and sex. Why do guys think women are oblivious to their bullshit?

It was the longest night in America. I got in bed beside Nia and went to sleep.

REFLECTION

"Hello, Mrs. Gladys, I won't be in today. I called a sub last night, not sure if they picked the assignment up yet," I said on the phone.

Last night seemed like yet another crazy dream. I looked over and saw Kade still passed out on the couch. I left the key on the table so that he could lock up. I was dropping Nia off at my mama's house. I did not want to take her to a hospital.

I don't know why I felt drawn to go visit Snow, but I just had to. I didn't need Coia's or Nikki's approval. It was the right thing to do.

I parked in the garage and headed inside Mercy Hospital. Part of me expected to see Keith running to her rescue to make sure she was alright. When I got to the information desk, I almost forgot her first name. The wife yelled it so many times in the hallway it should have been imprinted on my brain.

"Good morning, can you tell me what room Tamara Snow is in?" I asked.

She was on the fourth floor in room 4014. I took the elevator up, having no idea what I was going to say to her. Coia had no idea of her condition. I felt completely sick. I went to a nearby restroom and threw up. I just needed to get the nerve.

Snow lay completely still. Her eyes were closed. Half of her face was bandaged up. I did not want to wake her. Poor thing! She came to a new town excited about a teaching job and was gulped up by a predator, Keith.

Her eyes fluttered then opened slightly. "Belle, what are you…" She could not finish her sentence. She looked horrible. I did not mean any of the shit I said about her. It was the jealousy talking. Snow was a beautiful lady and a promising teacher.

"Hey, Tamara, don't try to talk. I'm sorry for everything," I said.

It was the first thing that came to my lips. Atonement was therapeutic. I walked over and grabbed her fragile hand. The other one was all crushed up. There was a chair near her bed. I sat down and continued.

"He isn't worth any of this. You deserve better," I added.

She did her best to answer, "I…I know. I'm sorry, your baby." Snow cried. She cried for Mia. We both were in the hospital crying together. I didn't want to hurt her hand. I felt my hand squeezing harder.

Her sister and mom, I assumed, walked in the room. I got up quickly so her mom could sit down.

I wiped my eyes. "Tamara, we need you to get better. Your kids miss you," I said.

"I'm a coworker. I just wanted to make sure she was okay," I stated to her mother.

They thanked me for coming, and I left. It was heartbreaking seeing her lying in that hospital bed. I think the therapy sessions were working. I was proud of myself.

I was disgusted with Keith. The trail of carnage he left was unforgivable. I bounced back after his bullshit, but Snow couldn't. If she pulls through, I will show her how to purge his stupid, useless ass.

Kade had gotten up and left two messages. I didn't hear my phone at all. I wasn't sure what I wanted to say to him. Eventually, I will get over it. For now, I was taking a page out of his book. He would get a call when I was good and damn ready.

The school board was my next stop. I went to see if Meredith was there. I had told her my story. But she needed to know about Snow's story. This behavior could not continue, and this man was supposed to be a leader.

It was a little after lunch when I arrived. Meredith's secretary informed me that she was out in the field. She gave me a sticky note to leave a message. The sticky note wasn't large enough to say what needed to be said. I asked her for a larger piece of paper. I sat in the lobby and wrote every detail necessary to get my point across.

Sure, I made adult choices to fuck with Keith. Of course, Snow did too. But he took advantage of our naivety and inexperience. That part was not okay. He used his position to manipulate. When he was done using us, he discarded women like trash. I did not want to see him do that to another young teacher. I felt my phone vibrate in my purse. "Mama, hey, what y'all up to?" I asked.

She told me the long drawn-out story about my daddy having another episode with his dementia. I told her that I would be right over. "No, no, girl, I want a break from all of that. I wanted you to meet me and Nia for lunch today. You already have the day off from work," she suggested.

I had done two good deeds for the day. Lunch with my favorite ladies seemed like a wonderful idea. Mama recommended an Italian restaurant in downtown Miami.

Parking was horrible. The lobby was full of people. I did not know this restaurant was so popular in the middle of the day. It was a very festive environment. I was dressed nice, but I should have really spruced myself up before getting here. It was just lunch with Mama and Nia, so I did not give it much thought. Nia spotted me first and ran up to me. "Mama, me and Mimi waiting over here." We walked over together where I saw everybody. What the hell was going on?

Coia, Nikki, Mama, Nia, and Jennifer were all waiting for me.

"Hey, you guys are supposed to be working. What are y'all doing here?" I asked. It was a nice surprise, but I was thoroughly confused.

Mama took the lead and explained why we were there. "Celeste, the last couple of months have been rough on you. We just wanted to get together and have a special lunch to celebrate you," she said.

The waiter came over to seat us. We were in a private room. There were more chairs and space than we really needed. Yet I was not going to complain.

I guess it was the only seating they had available. I went along with it. It was a great time to tell the ladies collectively that I went to see Snow in the hospital. They were all shocked. I explained that she was in bad shape and had a long road to recovery. They all gave their input. But everyone applauded me for being the bigger person.

"I guess that was nice. Didn't you just tell her you were going to kill her yesterday?" Coia said. She chuckled a little bit.

"The Lord is working on me," I exaggerated.

Just as the waiter was bringing in our salads, Kade walked in. Was this man stalking me?

What the fuck? I was having lunch with my girls and my baby; I did not want to see his indecisive ass. One minute, he wants to get reacquainted; the next, he wants to fuck his coworker.

Kade came over and sat by me.

"Hey, how is everybody doing?" he asked then reached over to Nia and kissed her forehead.

"Kade, what are you doing here?" I asked.

It was going to take a hell of a lot more than him paying for our lunch to get back on my good side!

"I came here looking for you actually," he said. As soon as he said that, six shades of chocolate-black men filed into the room and surrounded me. They began to sing their own version of the Freddy Jackson's "You Are My Lady" in a cappella. I was flattered and confused. When they finished, they all took a knee. Kade got up, pulled a rectangular-shaped box from a gift bag, and took a knee between me and Nia.

"Celeste Sincere Belle, you and Nia are my world. You make me better, you make me whole. I could not imagine my world without you in it. The first time that I saw you, I wanted you to be my queen. I will always love you, babe. Would you AND Nia do me the honor of marrying me?" he asked.

Kade opened the box from the gift bag. He put a beautiful gold ring on Nia's finger. He put a two-karat diamond ring on my finger. Then he pulled out a gold necklace that had another small ring on it. He put the chain around my neck.

"This ring is for Mia, who is no longer here. But I wanted you to have a wedding ring for her too," he said with a tear running down his face.

I lost it completely. I could not get the words out because I was crying so hard. There was not a dry eye in the house. The marriage proposal to me, Nia, and Mia was beyond touching.

I nodded because I could not get the words out. Kade and I stood up at the same time and hugged. Loud applause and whistles of celebration filled the room.

I could not believe it. He was missing in action yesterday planning this proposal dinner. I was so mean to him. Six shades of black sat down and joined us for dinner. It was amazing. I had not been this happy EVER! I had a moment of sadness and guilt that Mia was not part of it. Coia, Nikki, Jennifer, even Mama could not stop crying. "That's enough, crybabies," I joked.

"Okay, y'all, this is a celebration. No more crying," I demanded.

"We are getting married. I will be Mrs. Capshaw," I said aloud.

"Mama, you gotta buy me a wedding dress. I'm getting married too," Nia said.

She said it loud enough for the whole room to hear her. Laughter erupted all over the room. Of course, I'm getting my baby a wedding dress.

After the celebration, everyone parted ways. Mama offered to keep Nia to give me and Kade some private time. Kade interceded and insisted that he spend some time with me and Nia.

We rode home like a little family, just the three of us. Things were going great. I was not going to let anyone ruin it.

I reflected back to what Mama said. I needed to move. Kade and I spent the night looking at condos and houses for us. He agreed that a change would be good for us all.

DESERVING

Meredith called me very early.

"First I wanted to say congratulations for getting into the assistant principal's program. I support you fully. You will make a great educational leader," she informed me.

I saw the email but did not expect to get into the leadership program with everything that I disclosed about Keith. The comeback is ALWAYS greater than the setback! I felt accomplished.

I smiled from ear to ear on the other end of the phone. It was unexpected, awesome news. Meredith went on to notify me that something was being done about Keith. She could not tell me what exactly. But she did explain there was conversation with the superintendent about his inappropriate behavior.

Things were almost back to normal. Keith had been put on probation pending a thorough investigation. During the summer months, districts make a lot of changes. I had a feeling that Keith would be one of those changes. Snow and I had been exchanging emails. She was doing better. I did not mention Keith's name in either email. I was genuinely happy that she was doing better.

Two months had passed since Kade proposed. He gave me all the space and time that I needed to get my life back on track. I saw no reason to wait. We had known each other for four years. We decided to just go ahead and do it!

"Mama, I need your help. We have to pull a wedding together in a matter of two weeks," I asked.

We didn't want a fantasy wedding or extravagant destination wedding, just something simple. I had a wedding dress sitting in my closet for no reason at all. We went to a consignment shop a year ago.

I saw it and had to have it. I knew I would get married one day in life. It was the best fifty dollars I ever spent. I had no shame in wearing it.

"What's y'all rush, Celeste? I gotta see what I'm working with first," she said.

Her grouchy response actually meant "yes."

In addition to planning a hurried wedding, we were also looking for a place to stay. "Oh, by the way, any word from Big Mama?" I asked.

"Slow down, you have too much going on. Yes, I talked to Big Mama. I will plan the wedding. You go find a place, and leave me the hell alone, 'cause you getting on my damn nerves, li'l girl," she insisted.

Kade and Nia were the worst real estate agents ever! We had seen at least seven houses. Nia complained it was too hot every time we got out of the car to look at a house. Kade had no opinion at all. We had one more house to see.

"I don't care where we live as long as we have rooms, beds, and a kitchen. What's wrong with your house? It's nice," Kade inquired.

I refused to get into the voodoo feud my neighbors had going with my family. He would never understand. He would probably run away from it all. So I had to have a clever comeback.

"The old house has too many bad memories, and I want a fresh start, if that's not too much to ask," I cried. Kade kissed my hand and hugged me. That was code for…he would be more proactive in looking for our home.

We drove to a diverse neighborhood. It had beautifully manicured yards, white fences, and long sidewalks. The houses were amazing. I was unsure if we could afford such a nice neighborhood. Lord knows teachers don't make a lot of money, especially teachers in Florida. They pay the second-lowest salaries for teachers in the country. That is a fucking shame! My insurance money would pay for down payment and closing costs. Kade's attorney salary would qualify us both for the loan.

The realtor met us at the property. Once we went inside the split-level, open-house layout, I knew it was our home. I loved it! Nia even liked the house. She had already claimed her room. Kade walked around, knocked on the walls, ran water, opened the garage, and examined the AC unit. After we got his stamp of approval, the realtor told us she would write up the contract immediately.

We were so excited. It was our first couple "thing." Nia was even excited. I could see us getting a small fluffy puppy and walking him in the neighborhood.

I could check that off my major list of things to do. I asked Kade to drop me off at my mom's house so that I could assist her with wedding planning.

"You sure about that? I will have the car, and you will be stuck with Denise Belle. Shit can get ugly fast with the two of you," Kade said laughing.

We pulled into her driveway. I was surprised to see Coia, Jennifer, and Nikki there. I guess they were helping Mama too. Nia and I jumped out of the car to join the party.

"Hey, guys, we came to join you ladies," I said.

They were knee-deep in sheer tulle, centerpieces, and decorative flowers. I had my own designing crew. The ladies were focused on their individual tasks. I went to the kitchen and whipped up some deviled eggs, fried chicken wings, and sweetish meatballs. They were working hard to give me a great wedding. I wanted to at least give them a yummy meal. After I set the food on the table, I put some wine coolers in the freezer.

"Alexa, play 'Wobble,'" I requested.

Everyone in the room was yelling for Alexa to play their favorite songs.

We did the "Wobble," "Cha Cha Slide," "Electric Slide," "Cupid Shuffle" until we fell out. Coia turned the music down. "Okay, y'all ready?" she asked.

We all knew where this was going. Another crazy story. This girl was crazy as hell.

"So I never told you this part of my life, right? A year or two ago, I went down to the Black College Reunion in Daytona. That's nothing new because we always go. Fine. This time, I went to work. This dude paid me, TT, and Lil Bit to entertain his friends. We had a suite at the Marriot on the beach. Everything was cool. The music was vibing, plenty of food, the whole nine. Well, apparently, I was supposed to service dude's cousin. I went in the room, got all ready to dance. Got my damn outfit on, looking like I stepped out of a music video. The cousin walks in with three chains and a wifebeater on. Here's the kicker: that nigga was hairy as fuck. Not your average hairy! I mean abnormal for any damn human. He had full chest hair connecting to the full back hair, over the shoulder, like he had on a fucking wolf suit. I was sick as a dog. The nigga tried to touch me, and I jumped on the bed with both feet then on to the floor and headed for the door. I took that damn money, all $300, and handed that shit back to the dude. He was like, 'What's wrong, baby? Everything okay?' I told his ass, 'Look, I can't do it. This nigga too damn hairy for me. It's creeping me the fuck out.' By then, the hairy guy came out of the room talking shit. 'Bitch, what you talking 'bout, fuck you.' I cursed his Wilderilla-looking ass out. But wait… His cousins started joking this muthafucka out. His homeboy was like, 'You know we call that nigga Bomonkgunni, baby. That's a baboon, monkey, and gorilla mixed together.' Oh god, why did he say that? Then the hairy dude started calling me names. I kept hearing them chant 'Bomonkgunni.' He was *so* damn mad. He stormed out the room like a little-ass kid. They kept joking his ass out! I didn't even have to go in on him. His boys was killing his ass with the jokes. The guy that paid me said, 'Cuz is hairy as a muthafucka.' He laughed so hard that he fell on the couch behind him. I was like, 'Duh, you knew that shit, that's why you had to pay somebody for his ass.' One of the guys said, 'We told that nigga to go see a doctor about that shit.' I asked the dude, 'Then why the fuck did y'all hook me up with Harambe the Gorilla?' The whole damn room fell out again. He did let me keep the money, though," Coia finished.

My mama stared at her in disbelief. "We gone all have to pray for you, you need the Lord," she advised. Mama walked out of the room.

We were used to her outlandish stories. The three of us laughed at her ridiculous ass. As usual, we had *so* many questions. The shit that happens to her is unreal.

"So you telling me you went to the Black College Reunion as woman of the night or a damn stripper?" I asked in tears. I literally rolled on the floor.

Nikki and Jennifer looked at her with disappointment. They were also laughing. Nikki could not hold it any longer.

"You gone fuck around and lose your teaching certificate on some dumb shit. You know the shit you do ain't normal, right?" she asked.

Coia did not give a damn about anybody judging her. "Bitch, I had to make my damn paper, and I would do it again minus the gorilla," Coia clapped back.

"You are too old for this buffoonery, Coia," Jennifer stated.

Coia asked Alexa to play "City Girls Twerk" and started shaking her ass, showing off her moves.

"I ain't too old to twerk this ass though," Coia said. She continued dancing.

BLISS

Nothing was more breathtaking than a sunny blue Miami morning on the beach. I could hear my mom on the phone with the caterers giving instructions. Everything seemed so unreal. The wedding was at 6:00 p.m. It was a sunset wedding, so we wouldn't burn to death in heat.

In all the terrible things that I had been through in the last several months, I just may get my "happy ending." My life has been far from a fairy tale, but today, I felt like Cinderella. In a few short hours, I was going to marry the man who has stood by me and all my massive mistakes. He never judged me or treated me unfairly. I don't deserve him. The "old" me didn't deserve him, but the "new" me does! My therapy sessions have been a lifesaver. I even invited Dr. Allen to the wedding.

South Beach was gorgeous. It was the perfect setting for a wedding. The two-toned turquoise water kissed the white sands of the Miami shore. The sun reflected hypotonic light on the blue ocean. It's a splendor that few Floridians really appreciate. It was supposed to be a small intimate wedding on the beach. We had gotten to the beach early to set up. Kade and his fraternity brothers set up the arch on the beach and the chairs. They were taking advantage of the beach setting, snapping selfies and running in the shallow water puddles. Nikki and Jennifer decorated the arch with flowers and tulle. Coia and I set the chairs how we wanted them.

Mama directed and ordered us all around. She had to leave early to get Big Mama from the bus station. Big Mama refused to fly with her many superstitions.

"Mama, we have to get dressed. Why don't you get Jerald to pick her up?" I suggested.

Mama listened for a change and called my brother to go get Big Mama. That way, she could continue bossing all of us around. I did ask her to plan the wedding in two weeks. AND she did it!

The sunset beach package was a mere $395. It included the officiant, photographer, and chair decorations. *Good job, Denise Belle*, I thought.

Everything was set up beautifully. The bride-and-groom party split up to get dressed for the event. Mama went to double-check on the reception at the hotel where we were all staying. Time was flying! I had to get my baby dressed and get into my wedding dress. Mama met us inside the hotel suite.

"What the hell are you waiting for to get dressed? The wedding is in two hours," she said in a panic.

She was right. I had nervous energy and could not focus. Coia came flying in the door.

"I hope you're ready to have your face beat to the gods, bitch, 'cause I'm ready!" she yelled. She was crazy, but Coia was an expert at applying makeup professionally. I sat at the vanity and let her work her magic.

"So you learned to apply makeup from watching YouTube?" I asked. Coia took her makeup job seriously.

"Bitch, don't play with me unless you want to look like the Joker on your wedding day," Coia replied. I backed off. This was not the time for teasing. I did NOT want to look like the Joker today.

"Coia, I love you, but you have a filthy mouth, just filthy," Mama said.

That shit was hilarious. We cackled our asses off. Mama had some nerve. She curses like an angry truck driver.

"Keep still, you fucking up my concealer." Coia nudged me. With all the laughter, I didn't focus on the makeup. Suddenly, I turned and looked in the mirror. I was speechless. I was beautiful. The brows and eyelashes were flawless. The brown shades on my face were complimentary and unblemished. Coia did it!

She unclipped my hair. It was a jet-black deep wave with a part in the middle. The hair hung loosely down to my breasts. Coia fluffed the hair then applied mousse to add sheen and freshness. I never doubted my best friend. She put the cherry on top by placing the tiara on my head.

"Mommy, you look like a princess," Nia said. Before I could tell her thank you, Jennifer whisked Nia away to get her dressed. We had one hour before the wedding. Coia and Nikki helped me get into my consignment dress. We unzipped it, and I stepped into it. They pulled it up then zipped it. It was a fit and flare lace gown. It had a medium train with pearl buttons that ran up the center of the back. The dress displayed my hourglass figure down to the knee, where it flared out in a one-foot radius. It was sleeveless. Miami was too hot for long-sleeve lace. No way! I had to walk in beach sand, so the dress could not be too heavy or long.

The closer I was to being ready, the faster time moved. Mama back came in and almost broke down in tears. She added the veil on to the tiara. That made her weep. "Celeste, you have been through so much. It does my heart good to see you happy. I'm so proud of you for not giving up, baby," Mama said. She hugged me. We had a moment.

Nia entered the room in a mini wedding dress. It was the cutest thing I had ever seen. She looked like a bride baby doll, the kind you keep in the box as a collector's item.

The entire bridal party was dressed with fifteen minutes to spare until the actual ceremony.

The guests were arriving. Mama was directing and seating people while the wedding party prepared to start. I was so grateful to have wonderful friends and family to assist me.

The sand was calming between my toes. I probably should have had the dress altered shorter. The most unique part of this beach wedding was that we didn't have on any shoes. It was kind of corky and fun. It was a sunset wedding, so we wouldn't burn to death in heat. The ocean mist gave the atmosphere a cooler effect.

It was time. Kade was in place with his guys standing beside him. The music started, and the ladies went down the trail one by one. Nia stole the show with her beautiful ensemble. She had three flowers on both sides of the aisle then went and stood by Coia.

Everyone stood up and waited for me to come down the trail. I was nervous even though I was among family and friends. The last time we were all together like this was for Mia's funeral. My Mia. I missed her so much.

The music changed, and I headed down the trail smiling and focused on my one reason for being here, Kade. He was gorgeous! That beard was lined up like he was in a magazine. His brown skin complemented his white tux. The suit fit like it was designed for him only. I was the luckiest woman in the world. Six foot two never looked so good. He looked at me. I looked at him. We could not take our eyes off each other. I did not even scan the guests.

My brother gave me away because my daddy was too far gone. His dementia was so bad he couldn't remember who I was. Kade grabbed my hand. His eyes were watery. Awwww, my babe was emotional. I wiped his face with my hand. His grip became more firm. The two of us then turned to face the officiant. We could see the sunset over the blue ocean, unbelievably stunning. The officiant read his vows, and we agreed. Neither one of us was able to write vows without breaking down. We went with the simple solution. When he said the magic words "I now pronounce you Mr. and Mrs. Kade Capshaw," we hugged and kissed like we were the only two people on the beach.

Kade and I turned to face the guests and bowed. As I looked out into the audience, I saw all my friends and family. We exchanged smiles and hugs. There were some people whom I did not recognize immediately.

The neighbor Aurelia showed up. I did not invite her. She had a gift wrapped in all black paper with black ribbons and a black bow. It was strange. I did not dare reach out for that box. I remember when Mrs. Jackson gave me the Amazon box, my life was destroyed.

I felt a hand on my back. It was Big Mama. She moved with the speed of a cheetah. She positioned herself in front of me. "I'll take that," Big Mama said. She took the box and recited a few words over the box.

Big Mama then shoved the box back into Aurelia's chest with force. She said something in Creole that I did not quite understand. Big Mama discreetly waved for security to come over. "Make sure this trash gets to her car. If she so much as walks in the wrong direction, please alert the police," Big Mama said with force.

Kade did not pay much attention to what was going on. He was greeting guests.

Mama and I gave each other a look like we had just dodged a bullet. "That bitch thought she was going to avenge her sister's death by bringing that bullshit to my daughter's wedding," Mama stated.

I hugged Big Mama for two solid minutes. I was so glad to have her in my life. This dark ritual stuff is such a vicious cycle. The thirst for revenge never ends.

We all headed to the reception at the hotel to eat, drink, and unwind. The DJ did our grand announcement. "Ladies and gentlemen, I introduce to you, Mr. and Mrs. Kade Capshaw." The crowd roared with applause and cheers.

It had been a long day. I was starving. I had not eaten in two days preparing for the wedding. Kade and I sat at our special wedding table. A waiter brought us both plates of sliced roast, scalloped potatoes, fruit, and green beans. Kade dipped his fork in his food and fed me. I think I ate my food and his. I was starving.

The DJ started to crank things up. We went on the dance floor for our couple's dance.

I leaned in his big strong chest to the beat of Whitney Houston's "I Believe in You and Me." We slow danced like we were in high school. Other couples joined in. This was such a beautiful song. *Today is absolutely perfect*, I thought as he led the dance steps.

We left the dance floor hand in hand after the song was over.

I saw a female's face that I could not quite place. Kade had no problem recognizing her. This was the same lady from Kade's office. She started heading toward us. Kade suddenly stood straight up and looked back at me with a puzzled look. Everyone around us was dancing, eating, and drinking.

The woman was about five foot five; she was the same attractive Hispanic woman with a large stomach. In fact, the stomach was in a perfectly round shape. She walked up to the both of us.

"Sorry I'm late, South Beach traffic is a bitch on the weekends. Congratulations to you both. Kade, did your new wife know our baby is due in two months?"

Every thought in the world went through my mind. I went back to when Kade did not answer my call that night. He knew she was pregnant then and did not say a fucking word. I guess the breakup was more complicated than I thought. This bitch was here to ruin my wedding. I couldn't hit her because she was pregnant.

"Now that you have made your little insignificant point, you can get the fuck out of here before I have security or Miami Police throw your ass the fuck out," I said to her. Kade was speechless for about one solid minute. Kade, looking shocked, asked, "Man, what that fuck wrong with you? Get the hell out of here with that bull-shit." He had the most stupid look on his face. He was caught. I thought I was done with this shit when I left Promise.

The pregnant tramp turned around and said to Kade, "You will be hearing from me soon. You just made the biggest mistake of your life."

ABOUT THE AUTHOR

Chauncey Nelson began her career as an educator in Florida, where she acquired her love for writing and educating students. Chauncey taught in a middle school setting for thirteen years as a language arts teacher and seven years as a school counselor. Chauncey received her master's degree from Nova Southeastern University and her undergraduate degree from the University of South Florida. She is a proud member of the sorority Sigma Gamma Rho Incorporated.

She began writing her debut novel after being jaded by the systematic promiscuity that prioritized over student learning. Twenty years in, it was an "eye-opening" experience for her to know how much educated folk compromise themselves for personal and professional gain.

Chauncey resides in Tampa, Florida, with her three children, Jacob, Jada, and Jordan. The true love of her life is her furry baby, Bo-Jay, the world's cutest Pomeranian. When she's not writing, she is counseling disadvantaged teens and promoting social awareness in her small groups.

You can connect with Chauncey on Facebook at facebook.com/Chaunceynelson, Instagram at Chauncey_queen_squad, LinkedIn at Chauncey Nelson.